THE
2020
goal-getting
GUIDEBOOK FOR MAKERS

by

JANET LEBLANC
PAPERANDSPARK.COM

Table of Contents

WELCOME!

Welcome to the 2020 edition of the Goal-Getting Guidebook for Makers! I'm thrilled that you've decided to embrace your numbers along with me this year.

In this workbook, we're going to do a LOT of number-crunching and data-scrutinizing together. It will be hard work, but oh so worth it!

If you've always told yourself that you're "not a numbers person", I encourage you to shift that mindset ASAP. Your numbers can tell you a wealth of information about your business. Becoming a "numbers whisperer" is the key to getting strategic about your time & productivity. We're going to work on that page by page, together. You can do this!

In this year's guidebook, we will reflect on past results and create an actionable plan for a profitable future. This dual-process of reviewing and planning helps you drill down into what's working and what's not working for your shop.

We will use this data to work smarter, not harder within our businesses. Listening to the data allows you to build a business that truly supports your life, rather than letting your business RUN your life.

I'm confident that following the process in this Guidebook will be a game-changer for your business! I'm so excited for us to get started!

Ready to put in the work? Cheers to a profitable 2020!

Janet

HOW TO GET THE MOST
OUT OF YOUR GUIDEBOOK

This Guidebook will help you review past results & set goals for the future from a **numbers-driven perspective.** As creatives, we sometimes like to skip over dealing with the data. Not today, my friend.

You likely got into this business because you had a **financial** goal. We are going to break down your big financial goal into smaller, manageable numbers. And then we're going to break those numbers down into actionable steps to get there.

Your Goal-Getting Guidebook includes three main sections:

PART 1: 2019 BY THE NUMBERS
First, we dig deep into what happened last year in your business. We will calculate a few helpful percentages and ratios to help you see what worked well or what flopped. Knowing the history of your business is the key to setting *realistic and attainable* financial goals for the future.

If you're a newer business or don't have much to report for 2019, that's totally fine. Fill out this info as best as you can and move on to goal-setting for 2020.

PART 2: 2020 GOAL-SETTING
This is the heart and soul of your Guidebook! We tackle goal-setting from all angles here. You will work through setting solid goals for net income, sales, expenses, and much more. We will drill down on your financial goals and see how they correspond to your products, profit margins, and order numbers.

After we set specific financial and numerical goals, we'll map those out over the year. We break down what *action steps* you will focus on each month to achieve those financial goals. The Guidebook includes helpful worksheets that you can consult throughout the year to see at a glance how you're progressing towards the goals you've set.

Part 2 culminates with turning your financial goals and focus points into a guide map for how you will run your business in 2020. There's no point to setting all these goals if you don't let them guide your work throughout the year. Let your goals be your guide!

PART 3: 2020 PROGRESS TRACKING
Don't lose sight of your financial goals throughout the year when things get busy. Use this part of your guidebook to track your progress each month.

ACCESS YOUR BONUS MATERIALS

Get the most out of this Guidebook by accessing bonus materials from Paper + Spark®. Follow the link below to get the corresponding spreadsheet version of many of the exercises in this guidebook. This is a great tool if you'd rather use built-in formulas to crunch the numbers for you!

 paperandspark.com/2020GGG/

Video tutorials and additional content are also available. Every now and then I will ask you to record a number or a statistic that you may not understand or know where to find. I also have several helpful videos provided for you.

LET'S WORK TOGETHER

Join me and a community of your fellow goal-oriented makers in my Facebook group here:

facebook.com/groups/goalgettingmakers/

We host a live plan-a-thon every January and work through exercises (many of them directly from this Guidebook!) together. There are also quarterly check-ins and other activities throughout the year, so if you like to do your number-crunching with some support, come join us!

In the Goal Getting Makers community, you can plan with me live, ask questions about how to calculate something, and figure out how to set smart goals with a community of like-minded makers. Let's goal-get together.

THAT'S IT. NOW IT'S TIME TO GET GOAL-GETTING!

part 1:
2019 BY THE NUMBERS

2019 BY THE NUMBERS

Setting and achieving smart goals for the new year begins with reviewing your financial results and stats from last year.

In Part 1 of this Guidebook, you will take a close look at what actually happened in terms of sales, expenses, orders, and more. You'll also calculate some helpful stats and metrics. Remember, if you're a newer business, just fill out Part 1 to the best of your ability. Even just a few numbers will help us in Part 2!

For now, I invite you to record these results without stress or judgement. Think of this simply as the foundation of your goal-setting process - it's your baseline. At the end of Part 1, you will take some time to ponder what worked and didn't work in 2019.

If you have the 2019 Guidebook, you may be tempted to compare your entries here to last year's book. That's totally fine! Building up this wealth of data and analyzing trends from year to year is part of the fun.

I will occasionally explain some of the statistics that we calculate together so that you understand why that stat is valuable. Remember, no need to judge your stats for now. Just understand what it means and let's go from there.

We will build off these results and brainstorm ways to **improve efficiencies, increase profitability, and grow your business** in Part 2. For now, creating your starting point is the important part!

If you ever have questions about how to find a stat or calculate something, remember to ask in the Goal-Getting community on Facebook.

facebook.com/groups/goalgettingmakers/

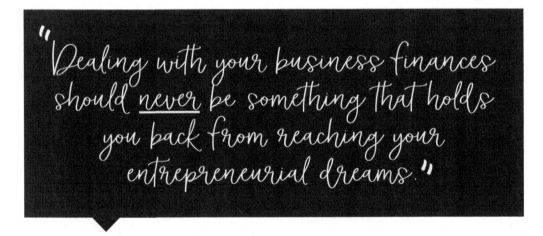

"Dealing with your business finances should never be something that holds you back from reaching your entrepreneurial dreams."

2019 BY THE NUMBERS

REVIEW YOUR FINANCIAL RESULTS

Let's begin by reviewing your financial results from 2019. Enter your total sales, expenses, and net income or loss (total sales minus total expenses) for each month of the year and for the entire year into the table below. You should be able to easily pull these numbers from your bookkeeping system. *If you need to update your 2019 books, now's the time!*

	TOTAL SALES	TOTAL EXPENSES	NET INCOME/ (LOSS)
JANUARY			
FEBRUARY			
MARCH			
APRIL			
MAY			
JUNE			
JULY			
AUGUST			
SEPTEMBER			
OCTOBER			
NOVEMBER			
DECEMBER			
2019			

2019 BY THE NUMBERS

REVIEW YOUR FINANCIAL RESULTS

Based on these financial numbers, we can calculate last year's profit margin ratio or percentage.

2019 NET INCOME= *taken from last page*	
TOTAL 2019 SALES= *taken from last page*	
2019 PROFIT MARGIN PERCENTAGE= *calculate this as net income divided by sales*	

WHAT DOES MY PROFIT MARGIN TELL ME?

Your profit margin is how much you're keeping in your pocket from every sale. So if you have a profit margin of 25%, that means for every $1 you make, you get to keep $.25.

The higher your profit margin, the more of each sale you are keeping to pay yourself, reinvest in your business, etc. A higher profit margin can mean you are running your business efficiently and not overspending. It can also mean your pricing strategy is optimized for profit.

The ideal profit margin really depends on your industry and business type. Most handmade businesses strive for a profit margin between 30-50%. Remember, this exercise is just to see where you are at. We will work on how to increase your profit margin, if needed, later in Part 2!

Do not be alarmed if your profit margin percentage is negative, especially if this was your first year in business.

2019 BY THE NUMBERS

REVIEW YOUR FINANCIAL RESULTS

Let's review the stats related to your sales. If you can't fill in the blanks for ALL of these questions, don't stress about it too hard. It's also fine to use estimates when necessary. You can usually find your number of orders in your Etsy or sales dashboard.

These numbers don't mean anything much by themselves, but knowing your average dollar amount per sale will help us set smarter goals for 2020.

NUMBER OF ORDERS =	
AVERAGE SALE AMOUNT PER ORDER = *Calculate this as your Total 2019 Sales (from the previous page) divided by your Number of Orders)*	
NUMBER OF ITEMS SOLD =	
AVERAGE ITEMS SOLD PER ORDER = *Calculate this as your Number of Items Sold divided by your Number of Orders*	

"A goal without a plan is just a wish."

2019 BY THE NUMBERS

REVIEW YOUR FINANCIAL RESULTS

If you want to break down this info even further and you have this info readily available, you can divide up your sales and number of orders **by source.**

	ETSY	SOURCE 1	SOURCE 2	SOURCE 3	TOTAL (SHOULD MATCH PREVIOUS PAGE)
SALES TOTAL=					
NUMBER OF ORDERS=					
AVERAGE SALE AMOUNT PER ORDER =					
NUMBER OF ITEMS SOLD =					
AVERAGE ITEMS SOLD PER ORDER =					

Do you notice anything interesting when comparing your different sales venues? Does one particular source seem to have a higher average sale amount per order than the others?

2019 BY THE NUMBERS

PRODUCTS

Let's take a look at the products and product categories you offered in your shop. What product or category sold the most in terms of **number of items sold**? If you sell one-of-a-kind items, you may need to consider the overall broader category type of your items (like earrings, rings, etc.). On the other hand, if you re-make the same items over and over again, you can list the specific products that sell best.

To calculate your percentage of total sales for each product, divide the number of items sold by the total number of items sold in 2019.

	PRODUCTS OR CATEGORIES	NUMBER OF ITEMS SOLD	% OF TOTAL SALES
1			
2			
3			
4			
5			
6			
7			
8			
9			
10			
	ALL OTHER PRODUCTS		
	TOTAL ITEMS SOLD IN 2019=		

2019 BY THE NUMBERS

PRODUCTS

Now shift gears just slightly - What product or product category made the most in **sales dollars**? These may not be the same as the items that sold the most in quantity from the previous exercise. You may sell more units of a low-priced item, but fewer sales of a higher-priced item bring in more total dollars.

List your top 10 highest grossing (biggest money making) products or categories below. Divide that amount by your total sales in 2019 (from page 10) to get your percentage of total sales.

	PRODUCTS OR CATEGORIES	TOTAL DOLLARS SOLD	% OF TOTAL SALES
1			
2			
3			
4			
5			
6			
7			
8			
9			
10			
		ALL OTHER PRODUCTS	
		TOTAL SALES DOLLARS IN 2019=	

If you're a visual person, express your sales in a color-coded pie chart on the next page. You can highlight each product or category a certain color in your table above, then fill in your pie chart appropriately. This gives you a great visual representation of how your sales are broken up and what products are supporting your bottom line. We'll use this to set goals in 2020.

2019 BY THE NUMBERS

PRODUCTS

SALES BY ITEM ORDERS

SALES BY DOLLAR AMOUNT

2019 BY THE NUMBERS

EXPENSES

Let's take a moment to breakout our total 2019 expenses (you recorded this way back on page 9) into spending categories. We will use this info to set a budget for our business in 2020. Don't stress too much about filling out these categories with 100% accuracy; overall rounded numbers are fine. Calculate your percentage of total expenses by taking that one category and dividing it by your total expenses in 2019. There is space to enter your own specific expense categories as well.

EXPENSE BREAKDOWN	TOTAL AMOUNT SPENT	% OF TOTAL EXPENSES
RAW MATERIALS & SUPPLIES		
ETSY FEES		
PAYPAL FEES & OTHER FEES		
SHIPPING & PACKAGING		
ADVERTISING		
APPS & SOFTWARE		
OFFICE EXPENSES		
PROFESSIONAL SERVICES		
EDUCATION & TRAINING		
TOTAL 2019 EXPENSES		

2019 BY THE NUMBERS

KEY PERFORMANCE INDICATORS & MORE

Let's wrap up our REVIEW by recording some of last year's **key performance indicators**, or KPIs.

KPIs give you a bit more info about how a certain sales venue, product, or marketing effort is working in your business. We've already calculated a few important KPIs, like your profit margin percentage.

Again, these numbers don't mean much by themselves, but they can be useful for creating a baseline and setting goals to improve.

Here are a few KPIs we will consider:

- Social media stats
- Views and visitors
- Conversion rates
- Bounce rate
- Average time spent on site

It's okay to make a mental note of which numbers you feel need improvement for now, but I encourage you to record this info without stress or anxiety. We'll decide which ones we want to improve on at the end of Part 1, and build a plan to do that in Part 2.

Alongside this quantitative data, we will record some other useful non-numeric data, including the following:

- Traffic sources & referrals
- Popular search terms
- Most popular listings

It's important to take note of both quantitative and qualitative info to analyze the health of our business and get the full picture.

With this data in our toolkit, we'll have a solid foundation to set smart, actionable goals to lead the way to success in 2020.

2019 BY THE NUMBERS

KEY PERFORMANCE INDICATORS & MORE

Social Media

Time to think about some social media stats! This gives us a baseline against which to track your progress in 2020. You only need to fill in the blank for sources that are important to you as a business owner. Ignore everything else.

	FANS/FOLLOWERS/NUMBERS as of 12/31/2019
FACEBOOK PAGE	
FACEBOOK GROUP	
INSTAGRAM	
TWITTER	
YOUTUBE	
PINTEREST	
SNAPCHAT	
EMAIL	
BLOG SUBSCRIBERS	

2019 BY THE NUMBERS

KEY PERFORMANCE INDICATORS & MORE

Conversion Rate

Let's review last year's conversion rate. Your conversion rate tells you how many of your shop or site visitors you successfully converted into a sale. You want this number to be as high as possible, keeping in mind average e-commerce conversion rates can vary, but are usually around 2-3%. A conversion rate of 2% means that for every 100 visitors that come to your shop, 2 will actually order something.

Conversion rate is usually calculated as follows:

Conversion rate = number of sales in a given time period / number of visitors within the same time period

Note that you always want to use *visitors* rather than *views*. In your Etsy shop dashboard, this shows up as "Visits". In Google Analytics, you could use your "Users" number.

Don't worry too much about fixing a low conversion rate right now. Let's just set a baseline for how you have been converting thus far. This will help us set some smarter goals for 2020.

You can calculate your Etsy shop's conversion rate based on numbers available in your Etsy stats. If you have Google Analytics or some other stats for another shop, you can calculate those conversion rates here as well. Note that we will discuss Google Analytics (and how to find your number of visitors) on page 24.

ETSY SHOP CONVERSION RATE:	
_____ **SITE CONVERSION RATE:**	
_____ **SITE CONVERSION RATE:**	
_____ **SITE CONVERSION RATE:**	

2019 BY THE NUMBERS

KEY PERFORMANCE INDICATORS & MORE

You can also calculate your conversion rate per listing on Etsy. In your Stats dashboard, scroll down to the "Listings" area to see your most viewed listings.

TOP 10 MOST VISITED LISTINGS ON ETSY

	PRODUCT	VISITS	ORDERS	CONVERSION RATE =orders/visits	REVENUE
1					
2					
3					
4					
5					
6					
7					
8					
9					
10					

2019 BY THE NUMBERS

KEY PERFORMANCE INDICATORS & MORE

If you have the correct data to do this for your own site or another sales venue outside of Etsy, there is space to do so here.

TOP 10 MOST VISITED PRODUCTS ON _____ SITE

	PRODUCT	VISITS	ORDERS	CONVERSION RATE =orders/visits	REVENUE
1					
2					
3					
4					
5					
6					
7					
8					
9					
10					

2019 BY THE NUMBERS

KEY PERFORMANCE INDICATORS & MORE

Traffic Sources

Where is your Etsy site or shop traffic coming from? Make sure to drill down on each main source. How much traffic is coming from Etsy, and specifically Etsy search? How much traffic comes from searches outside of Etsy, like Google? How successful have your social media campaigns been at driving traffic to your shop?

Referral Sites

Check out your referral sites listed. List your referral sites below.

2019 BY THE NUMBERS

KEY PERFORMANCE INDICATORS & MORE

Search Terms

List your top 10-20 most used popular search terms for the year.

	SEARCH TERM
1	
2	
3	
4	
5	
6	
7	
8	
9	
10	
11	
12	
13	
14	
15	
16	
17	
18	
19	
20	

2019 BY THE NUMBERS

KEY PERFORMANCE INDICATORS & MORE

Google Analytics

Google Analytics (GA) is another wealth of info for you. If you have GA tracking set up for your site or shop, you will be able to fill out the following pages with 2019 data. If you don't have GA set up for your site yet, get it set up ASAP so you can start tracking this data! Again, make sure you change your settings to view data for the entire year.

Fill in the charts below. These stats are just the tip of the HUGE iceberg of analytical data GA provides. You are welcome to spend some time exploring your GA dashboard and drilling down for even more useful insights.

UNDER "AUDIENCE"	
USERS	
BOUNCE RATE	
% NEW/RETURNING VISITOR	

UNDER "ACQUISITION"	
% TRAFFIC FROM SOCIAL & BOUNCE RATE	
% TRAFFIC FROM ORGANIC SEARCH & BOUNCE RATE	
% TRAFFIC FROM DIRECT & BOUNCE RATE	
% TRAFFIC FROM REFERRAL & BOUNCE RATE	

UNDER "BEHAVIOR"	
PAGEVIEWS	
UNIQUE PAGEVIEWS	
AVERAGE TIME ON PAGE	
PAGES WITH MOST PAGEVIEWS	

2019 BY THE NUMBERS

KEY PERFORMANCE INDICATORS & MORE

What do these KPI's actually mean?

Curious what some of these KPIs actually mean? Let's discuss.

AUDIENCE

- Your number of users are your unique visitors during the time period. Their bounce rate is how many of these users took no further action and left after viewing this page. A high bounce rate means your visitors are literally saying "bye" when they get to your page.

ACQUISITION

- Where is your traffic actually coming from - social media, search engines, direct links (like from your email campaigns), or referrals from other sites on the internet?

- What's the quality of traffic from each source? Sources with higher bounce rates mean that traffic may be coming to your site, but they are leaving as soon as they get there. This data will tell you which sources are driving good quality traffic and poor quality traffic.

BEHAVIOR

- How long do your visitors spend on certain pages? Which pages get the most views?

2019 BY THE NUMBERS

KEY PERFORMANCE INDICATORS & MORE

So far, I've been telling you to record your 2019 results without any judgement. Here's your permission to officially start judging yourself. Let's transition from calculating stats to thinking about what these stats are telling you and recalling how the year felt to you as the owner and operator of your shop.

We will review what worked in 2019 and what didn't. This will help you project how things will go in 2020 with more accuracy.

Remember, if you want to download a spreadsheet to crunch some of these numbers for you, you can do so here:

📎 paperandspark.com/2020GGG/

"When it comes to jokes, I Excel."

-SPREADSHEET HUMOR

2019 BY THE NUMBERS

R E V I E W

Now that you've crunched the numbers and calculated some KPIs, let's summarize all your important stats from prior pages in 2019 in one place. As you summarize, I want you to note whether you are satisfied or dissatisfied with that particular stat by answering "yes", "no", or "maybe" to whether this stat needs improvement. This will give us an idea of the focus points and specific areas you want to work on in 2020.

STATISTIC	2019 RESULT	NEEDS IMPROVEMENT?
PROFIT MARGIN PERCENTAGE		☐ YES ☐ NO ☐ MAYBE
AVERAGE SALE AMOUNT PER ORDER		☐ YES ☐ NO ☐ MAYBE
AVERAGE ITEMS SOLD PER ORDER		☐ YES ☐ NO ☐ MAYBE
CONVERSION RATE		☐ YES ☐ NO ☐ MAYBE
		☐ YES ☐ NO ☐ MAYBE
		☐ YES ☐ NO ☐ MAYBE
		☐ YES ☐ NO ☐ MAYBE

You may also have a few other things, financial or otherwise, that you know you want to pay attention to going forward. Fill out the below box accordingly.

STATISTIC	2019 NOTES	NEEDS IMPROVEMENT?
AVERAGE REVENUE GROWTH		☐ YES ☐ NO ☐ MAYBE
AVERAGE SPENDING GROWTH		☐ YES ☐ NO ☐ MAYBE
PRODUCT MIX		☐ YES ☐ NO ☐ MAYBE
REVENUE MIX		☐ YES ☐ NO ☐ MAYBE
AMOUNT OF TRAFFIC		☐ YES ☐ NO ☐ MAYBE
		☐ YES ☐ NO ☐ MAYBE
		☐ YES ☐ NO ☐ MAYBE

2019 BY THE NUMBERS

REVIEW - THE GOOD

What were your top three best-selling products?

What was your most profitable sales venue or event?

What things did you do particularly well when it came to how you ran your business or got things done?

2019 BY THE NUMBERS

REVIEW - THE GOOD

What strategies were worth your time, energy or money in 2019?
Reflect on this from all angles and perspectives using the categorized boxes below.

PRODUCT DEVELOPMENT

MARKETING EFFORTS

RELATIONSHIPS & COLLABORATIONS

PROCESSES & SYSTEMS

INVESTMENT IN TRAINING, EQUIPMENT, COURSES, TOOLS, ETC.

OTHER

2019 BY THE NUMBERS

REVIEW - THE BAD

What were your worst three products that wasted time, energy or money?

What venues or events wasted your time, energy, and money?

What things did you do not do so well when it came to how you ran your business? What did you keep putting off or fail to do?

2019 BY THE NUMBERS

REVIEW - THE BAD

What strategies were NOT worth your time, energy or money or FAILED in 2019?
Reflect on this from all angles and perspectives using the categorized boxes below.

PRODUCT DEVELOPMENT

MARKETING EFFORTS

RELATIONSHIPS & COLLABORATIONS

PROCESSES & SYSTEMS

INVESTMENT IN TRAINING, EQUIPMENT,
COURSES, TOOLS, ETC.

OTHER

2019 BY THE NUMBERS

REVIEW - HOW DID YOU SPEND YOUR TIME?

Think about how you spent the majority of your work time last year. When you got started on a typical work day (or evening, or whatever), what sort of tasks did you do? List out as many as you can think of below. Examples are: cutting fabric, sewing purses, sourcing materials at the fabric store, photographing listings, posting on Instagram, writing an email to my list, etc. Literally think of every type of activity you performed. This list will be long, but I promise there's a point to this we'll dive into later!

-
-
-
-
-
-
-
-
-
-
-
-
-
-
-
-
-
-
-
-

2019 BY THE NUMBERS

REVIEW - HOW DID YOU SPEND YOUR TIME?

Now I want you to examine each of these activities you listed on the previous page and categorize them as one of the following types of activities:

- Revenue-generating activity
- Momentum-building activity
- Maintenance activity or busy work

Revenue-generating activities directly lead you to making sales. This is the work you do that helps you make income. This may include listing a new product in your shop, crafting a sales email to your list, or answering a potential customer's question about creating a customized product.

Momentum-building activities help you build an audience and build buzz. These activities may not directly lead to sales, but they help you gain traction in your market. Momentum-building activities get traffic to your site and eyeballs on your products. They make your target audience aware of your brand.

Momentum-building activities should be focused and strategic. You want to be building a list of potential customers from your target market and getting the right eyeballs on your products. Examples could include pinning items to your shop Pinterest board, scheduling carefully curated content for your Facebook page, or writing a gift guide for your blog.

Maintenance activities are the daily grind of running your shop! These include some tasks you must to do keep your business running smoothly. Examples include packaging orders, reordering supplies, or doing your bookkeeping.

We have to be careful because maintenance activities can also include the less meaningful "busy work" of running a business. These are tasks that you may feel like you need to do, but they don't really generate sales, build marketing traction, or keep your business running smoothly. Examples could include checking your social media notifications, editing photos, or checking your Etsy stats.

What specific type of activity falls into which category will depend on your business.

Sometimes you may need to work backwards from a revenue-generating activity and still consider those "pre" activities to also be revenue-generating, but I want you to consider carefully their true value and the time you dedicate to them.

2019 BY THE NUMBERS

For example, a lot goes in to getting a new product listed for sale in your shop. Listing a product itself generates revenue because you can't make a sale without a product to buy in your shop!

Working backwards, photographing your new product is necessary to list it in your shop, so that could be considered a revenue-generating activity as well. However, editing your photos for hours on end trying to get it to *perfection* could be more of a delay tactic and a maintenance activity if your edit job isn't going to increase sales (getting it PUBLISHED is likely more important than getting it PERFECT!). The same goes for constantly tweaking and re-tweaking your keywords. At some point, you are better off moving on to a more effective activity.

How did you spend your time?

I want you to go through your list of how you spent your time last year on page 32 and highlight each activity a specific color, based on whether you identify it as a revenue-generating activity, a momentum-building activity, or a maintenance activity.

I WILL HIGHLIGHT REVENUE-GENERATING ACTIVITIES _____

I WILL HIGHLIGHT MOMENTUM-BUILDING ACTIVITIES _____

I WILL HIGHLIGHT MAINTENANCE ACTIVITIES _____

Don't think too long or hard about categorizing your activities in the "right" bucket. And don't judge yourself as you do this exercise either. There is no wrong or right here; we're just building awareness of how effectively and efficiently you spend your time in your business.

We'll use this list of activities and shift our focus to the most important ones when we build a plan for 2020.

2019 BY THE NUMBERS

REVIEW - PAYING YOURSELF

Were you able to pay yourself in 2019 from your business profits? If yes, how much?

Are you happy with the amount you did or did not pay yourself?

2019 BY THE NUMBERS

> *"Take a deep breath and sit back for a moment. All that hard work is about to pay off!"*

Whew! That was hard work. I know that sorting through, totaling up, and analyzing allllll those numbers takes a lot of energy. You did great! Your hard work will enable us to set smart goals for 2019. We can analyze trends, prepare for growth, build momentum, and work more efficiently in the new year.

Take a deep breath right now. If you feel really tuckered out from the work you just did - take a break too. It's okay to take a day or two off and get back to your creative work. Your goals will be waiting for you when you're ready! Just don't wait too long.

When you're ready to dive into the next step, we're going to move forward into the nitty gritty of setting real, concrete, specific financial goals for 2020. So grab your coffee, calculator, and your thinking cap, and let's get goal-getting!

Remember, you are welcome to join us as we work through these exercises and more LIVE in the Facebook group.

Prepare to work smarter, not harder!

 You can find the Facebook group at: facebook.com/groups/goalgettingmakers/

part 2:

2020 GOAL SETTING

2020 GOAL SETTING

Now comes the fun part!

We have thoroughly analyzed what happened in 2019. By now, you should have a solid grasp on what worked and what didn't work last year.

Now comes the fun part. In Part 2, we will set new financial goals based on what we've learned in Part 1. Part 2 begins with the most important goal of all - the goal of paying yourself for your hard work. I encourage you to think deeply about how much you want to pay yourself in 2020. We will build EVERYTHING around this goal to make sure it happens. Paying yourself is just THAT important!

We're going to work backwards from **big picture** to **daily to dos** to set our 2020 goals. These goals will guide your action plan for the new year as well. This might involve brainstorming ways to streamline how you get work done, drive more traffic, build your audience, and increase profitability.

As we set financial goals in Part 2, you may expose some weaknesses in your current business structure. These weaknesses will direct us to what you need to focus on most during the year to reach your new goals - I call these your "focus points" for the year.

As you unearth a new focus point, you can mark it on page 76 of the workbook. We'll build an action plan to work on each focus point at the end of Part 2.

2020 GOAL SETTING

PAYING YOURSELF

The first step of your financial goal planning for the new year is to determine **how much you want to pay yourself** in 2020. This is a super important financial number that we often ignore, or save until the end of the process.

Nope - I don't want you to figure out your goal net income for the year and then see how much of it you can pay yourself; I want you to know how much you want to pay yourself and build your entire business around the ability to do that. That is why we set this goal at the very beginning - so we can account for it in all of our other goals & budget.

Let's ease into this. Sometimes you may feel a bit icky thinking about paying yourself. I want to start the conversation by reminding yourself WHY you started this business to begin with.

Your big financial goals (and how much you want to pay yourself) first depend on your "why" - the reason you started your business. I want you to write down all your "whys" below.

Chances are your why involves at least one financial component - and that's a good thing. If you didn't write something down that involves money in some aspect, I want you to keep working backwards until you unearth a financial-related "why".

What is your why? Why did your start your business in the first place? What keeps you motivated?

2020 GOAL SETTING

PAYING YOURSELF

Now let's get down to the numbers. We begin the entire goal-setting process by setting your **take-home pay goal for the year**.

Take-home pay is the amount you would like to literally take out of your business account and put in your own pocket. That means this amount is after all your business expenses have been taken out of your sales.

Your take-home pay goal may be equivalent to your day job's salary. It may be the amount you need to take your family on a cruise for the holidays. It may be four, or five, or six-figures. There is no right or wrong amount, just remember your "why" and what's important to YOU. Write your take-home pay goal below.

Next, think about how much you'd like to have "left over" in your business bank account after you pay yourself. You usually don't want your biz bank account to have a balance of exactly zero in it. How much, after paying yourself and after accounting for all your business' other expenses, do you want to have as a cushion in your bank account for a rainy day or investment opportunity?

TAKE-HOME PAY GOAL:	$
CUSHION FOR REINVESTING IN BIZ:	$

We are going to base ALL our financial planning for 2020 around this goal of being able to pay yourself the amount above.

2020 GOAL SETTING

NET INCOME

TAKE-HOME PAY GOAL ⟶ NET INCOME GOAL

Let's continue to work backward from big picture to daily to dos. The next step of the goal-getting process is to figure out what you need your business' total net income to be for the year in order to pay yourself your goal take-home pay.

Recall that your net income is your total sales minus your total business expenses (not including the amount you pay yourself). You can think of your net income as the total amount you have left over from which to pay yourself and/or just leave in your bank account for a rainy day.

Ideally, you pay yourself from your net income and then also have some extra left over for a rainy day. If you add your take-home pay goal and your cushion for reinvesting amount together from the previous page, that gets you your net income goal. You can also add a bit to it if you want some more wiggle room.

MY 2020 NET INCOME GOAL IS: $

2020 GOAL SETTING

NET INCOME

TAKE-HOME PAY GOAL	→	NET INCOME GOAL	→	SALES GOAL & EXPENSE GOAL

Now we're going to take that net income goal and work backwards to break it down into your goal for both **total sales** and **total expenses** in 2020.

How do we figure that out? The best starting point is to look at last year's results that you recorded in Part 1.

What was your profit margin percentage in 2019? You determined this number back on page 10. Now what happens if you apply that number to your **net income goal** for 2020? We can do this with a little math - let me walk you through an example.

Example (also see box on next page): In 2019, I had total sales of $45,000 and total net income of $22,000. Thus, my profit margin percentage was 48.8%.

If my total net income goal for 2020 is $50,000, then I would divide $50,000 by 48.8% to figure out what my total sales would need to be to meet that goal.

$$\$50,000/48.8\% = \$102,459$$

If I continue to have a profit margin percentage of 48.8% next year, I'd need to make about $102,459 in sales to meet my net income goal of $50,000. This would mean expenses totaling $102,459 - $50,000 = $52,459.

Fill out the box on the next page with your numbers to calculate your sales & expense goals for 2020.

If you had a loss last year (and thus a negative profit margin percentage), use a positive profit margin percentage for this exercise. Keep reading for more info on what benchmark numbers you may use instead.

2020 GOAL SETTING

NET INCOME

TAKE-HOME PAY GOAL → NET INCOME GOAL → SALES GOAL & EXPENSE GOAL

EXAMPLE	YOUR BIZ
Total 2019 Sales = $45,000	TOTAL 2019 SALES =
Total 2019 Net Income = $22,000	TOTAL 2019 NET INCOME =
Profit Margin Percentage = $22,000/$45,000 = 48.8%	PROFIT MARGIN PERCENTAGE =
Total 2020 Net Income Goal = $50,000	TOTAL 2020 NET INCOME GOAL =
Total 2020 Sales Goal = $50,000/48.8% = $102,459	TOTAL 2020 SALES GOAL =
Total 2020 Expenses Goal = $102,459 - $50,000 = $52,459	TOTAL 2020 EXPENSES GOAL =

2020 NET INCOME GOAL OF $

DIVIDED BY 2019 PROFIT MARGIN PERCENTAGE OF   %

EQUALS A 2020 SALES GOAL OF $

...WHICH MEANS TOTAL 2020 EXPENSES EQUAL TO $

2020 GOAL SETTING
NET INCOME

TAKE-HOME PAY GOAL	→	NET INCOME GOAL	→	SALES GOAL & EXPENSE GOAL

Goal-setting is a bit of an art and a bit of a science. We just set a goal based on prior year data (numbers!). The evidence or trends we discover often repeat themselves. But they are just a starting point, particularly in the handmade industry where things are changing so quickly.

We just used the "profit margin ratio" method to work backwards to set your sales & expense goals for 2020, but this isn't the ONLY way to get there and the number is definitely up for some tweaking, especially if you had a loss or a one-off year last year.

THE PROFIT MARGIN RATIO METHOD
Do these sales and expense goals you just calculated seem reasonable to you?

Consider that your profit margin percentage may be drastically different in 2020. Remember, your profit margin depends on your expenses. It's safe to assume that as your sales increase, your expenses increase accordingly. But it's possible that in 2019, you had more/less expenses than you will in the future. Last year, you may have invested in new equipment or a bunch of supplies, and these expenses won't be duplicated in 2020. Or you may plan to invest more in 2020. It's not necessarily a one-to-one ratio, so if you need to adjust your profit margin ratio in this exercise, that's totally fine.

Your profit margin percentage can also depend on your product markup and your pricing. If you plan to raise your prices in the new year, that would increase your profit margin ratio as well, assuming expenses don't increase at a corresponding rate.

If having a consistently low profit margin percentage is something you're concerned about, and you want to spend more time working to improve it, make sure you circle "increasing profitability and profit margin" as one of your focus points on page 76.

FOCUS POINT ALERT

2020 GOAL SETTING

NET INCOME

USE COMMON SENSE
Setting your 2020 goals based on last year's profit margin ratio is simply a good starting point, but you don't have to end there. Feel free to adjust that total sales goal and total expenses goal based on your intuition, what you think will reasonably happen in 2020 and other factors.

WHAT IF I'M KIND OF NEW HERE?
I understand that the profit margin ratio method that we start with here is based solely on what happened last year. If you are a brand new business, you may feel a bit lost right now.

Don't get stressed about this, just do the best you can with any results you DO have under your belt.

If 2020 is your first big year of operations, I suggest you do a bit of recon and market research before setting your sales goal. This analysis can serve as a replacement for not having much prior year data on which to base your goals. Here are a few ideas:

- First, still do the 2019 exercises even if you have just a few sales or data points to enter. A little bit goes a long way.

- Check out other competing shops. On Etsy, we can often see how many sales other shops have under their belt. This is a good way to get a feel for how many orders an established shop in your niche has the potential for.

- Google "income reports" for Etsy shops or for your niche (ie, "income report for jewelry maker", etc.). Some shop owners who have been around the block for many years will actually publish sales reports on their blogs! This gives you another idea of what is achievable down the road.

- Talk to others in your niche about how they set goals and what they hope to achieve in 2020. I do not suggest going ask your favorite Facebook group how many items they sold or how much they made in 2019 (although some shop owners may be okay divulging that). However, a useful prompt may be to ask how much fellow shop owners hope to make in 2020. This is a good gauge for a starting point.

2020 GOAL SETTING

NET INCOME

- Remember that this is about **goal-setting**. It's not about predicting the future. Set goals that inspire and motivate you. Your net income goal may be a number that relates to meeting a specific personal or family goal. It may have nothing to do with your shop's past or the marketplace. How much do you need to or want to make with your business? How far can you push yourself? It's okay to set goals based on these factors rather than scientific data points.

If all else fails, remember that the typical handmade shop should ideally aim for a profit margin of 30-50%. Use a number in that range to apply to your take-home pay goal and set your sales goal.

TAKE-HOME PAY GOAL → NET INCOME GOAL → SALES GOAL & EXPENSE GOAL

MAKE IT A STRETCH BUT REALISTIC

I want your goal to inspire you! Let's go big or go home, as they say. Set a sales goal that will motivate you to work hard, but make it realistic. I don't want your goal to be so unattainable that you lose motivation to keep working towards it mid-year.

Jot down your final (and if necessary, adjusted) net income, sales, and expense goals for 2020 below.

2020 NET INCOME GOAL OF $

2020 SALES GOAL OF   %

...WHICH MEANS TOTAL 2020 EXPENSES EQUAL TO $

2020 GOAL SETTING

ORDERS

TAKE-HOME PAY GOAL → NET INCOME GOAL → SALES GOAL & EXPENSE GOAL → ORDERS GOAL

Our main focus now is to figure out how reach that all-important sales goal - what will it take to get there in terms of orders? How many customers do we need? What actions do we need to take to get there? Let's break this down as detailed as we can get!

Next, think about what your overall sales goal means for your actual number of sales (orders). We'll make some estimates based on last year's numbers and break it down by product category as well. Check out the example below, then fill in the right-hand column to work through the numbers for your business.

In 2019, I had 416 orders for a total of $45,000 in sales. My 2020 sales goal is $102,459. Based on prior year stats, I would need to get about 947 orders in 2020 to meet this goal, as calculated below.

EXAMPLE	YOUR BIZ
Total 2019 Sales = $45,000	TOTAL 2019 SALES =
Total 2019 Orders = 416	TOTAL 2019 ORDERS =
Average Sale Per Order = $45,000/416 = $108.17	AVERAGE SALE PER ORDER =
Total 2020 Sales Goal = $102,459	TOTAL 2020 SALES GOAL =
Total 2020 Orders Needed To Reach Goal = $102,459/$108.17 = 947.2	TOTAL 2020 ORDERS NEEDED =

2020 GOAL SETTING

ORDERS

TAKE-HOME PAY GOAL → NET INCOME GOAL → SALES GOAL & EXPENSE GOAL → ORDERS GOAL

If you want to break down this goal even further to match last year's results, you can divide up your sales and number of orders goals by source.

	ETSY	SOURCE 1	SOURCE 2	SOURCE 3	TOTAL (SHOULD MATCH PREVIOUS PAGE)
SALES GOAL PER SOURCE=					
ORDERS GOAL=					

Does the number of orders required to reach your goal seem reasonable and achievable for 2020?

If this number seems like a stretch, we can consider a few things as we make adjustments and add these to our focus points for the year - first, your average dollar amount per order, second, your conversion rate.

YOUR AVERAGE DOLLAR AMOUNT PER ORDER

One important stat to think about is the average dollar amount per order. Can you find ways to increase how much each customer spends on their order in 2020? Here are a few ideas that would help you do that:

- Increase your prices, especially for your best-selling items. Increasing your prices is the EASIEST way to increase your average dollar amount per order.

2020 GOAL SETTING

ORDERS

- Encourage customers to buy multiple items, rather than just one (suggest related products in your listings, buy one get one at a discount, etc.)

- Offer free shipping for orders over a certain amount

- Create gift sets of multiple items

- Link to related items that go well together to encourage them to buy something else

- Bundle items that often sell together and offer them for a slight discount

- Offer add-on items

- Charge a small upgraded fee for personalization, gift wrap, a handwritten note, etc.

If you can increase your average sale amount per order, then you don't necessarily need to make as many orders in 2020 to reach your goal. It's often easier to convince the same customer to just spend more money per order than it is to drive more traffic and get more orders, so focusing on increasing your average order value can be a worthwhile investment of your time.

If increasing your average dollar amount per order is something you want to focus on in 2020, make sure to circle it on your focus points chart on page 76.

FOCUS POINT ALERT

> " *Success is where preparation and opportunity meet.* "
>
> —BOBBY UNSER

2020 GOAL SETTING

CONVERSION RATE

TAKE-HOME PAY GOAL	→	NET INCOME GOAL	→	SALES GOAL & EXPENSE GOAL	→	ORDERS GOAL	→	VISITORS GOAL

YOUR CONVERSION RATE

Remember your conversion rate(s) that we crunched back in Part 1. Your conversion rate told you how many visitors it takes to convert to one sale (a 3% conversion rate means for every 100 visitors to your site, 3 actually order something).

Using last year's conversion rate, we can work backwards from the orders goal you just set to see how many visitors you would need to attain that number of orders. We can also assess if THAT number seems reasonable. If needed, you can brainstorm ways to increase your conversion rate to help you achieve your orders goal.

Recall that your conversion rate is usually calculated as your number of orders in a given time period divided by the number of visitors within the same time period. We can use last year's conversion rates (taken from page 19) and this year's order goals (taken from page 48) to see how much traffic you need to reach your sales goals.

	2019 CONVERSION RATES	2020 ORDER GOALS	VISITORS REQUIRED (=order goals/conversion rate)
EXAMPLE ETSY SHOP:	3%	947.2	947.2 / 3% = 31,573 visitors this year
ETSY CONVERSION RATE:			
SITE CONVERSION RATE:			
SITE CONVERSION RATE:			
SITE CONVERSION RATE:			

2020 GOAL SETTING

CONVERSION RATE

2020 VISITORS GOAL=

Does this amount of visitors seem attainable in light of last year's results and/or what you intuitively know about your business? If not, we have two options to consider.

First, we can work on increasing your conversion rate so that you turn more of your existing visitors into sales, without needing to necessarily drive MORE traffic to your shop. This would be like increasing your conversion rate from 3 sales for every 100 customers to 5 sales for every 100 customers.

Second, we can work with your existing conversion rate and brainstorm ways to drive MORE visitors to your shop. More traffic means more sales.

Basically, you want to consider whether you need more traffic or an increased conversion rate. Or you may opt to focus on both.

Either or both of these may be appropriate focus points on page 76 for your business this year if you need to reach new heights to hit your orders goal. Since driving traffic and increasing conversions are a common pain point, we'll also take a moment to do a little brainstorming on this topic right now.

2020 GOAL SETTING

CONVERSION RATE

TAKE-HOME PAY GOAL → NET INCOME GOAL → SALES GOAL & EXPENSE GOAL → ORDERS GOAL → VISITORS GOAL

WHAT ACTION STEPS CAN YOU TAKE TO INCREASE TRAFFIC TO YOUR SITE?

Keeping in mind how many visitors you had to your shop site last year, how can you drive more traffic? Take a look at where the majority of your traffic came from last year. What worked to get you visitors, and what didn't seem to work very well? What strategies can you put in action to increase visitors from those same sources? Think about the best ways you can sprinkle your link all around the interwebs!

What other marketing tactics could you try to gain traffic from new or different sources? Examples include guest posts on someone else's blog, sharing your product with an influencer, increasing your email marketing efforts, etc.

Increasing *traffic* is mostly about **quantity**. Increasing your conversion rate boils down to the **quality** of that traffic. We'll talk about that next.

2020 GOAL SETTING

CONVERSION RATE

TAKE-HOME PAY GOAL → NET INCOME GOAL → SALES GOAL & EXPENSE GOAL → ORDERS GOAL → VISITORS GOAL

WHAT ACTION STEPS CAN YOU TAKE TO INCREASE YOUR CONVERSION RATE?

Getting a ton of people into your shop can help increase sales. But let's work smarter, not harder - we want the RIGHT people putting eyeballs on your products. I'm talking about finding quality visitors. Five visitors who are looking for exactly what you're selling and are ready to buy are better than fifty aimless browsers.

How can you work on making sure the RIGHT visitors are landing in your shop? Brainstorm some ideas here. This may mean tweaking your keywords & tags to get MORE specific, changing photographs, copy or branding to draw in the right type of buyer, etc.

Brainstorm a list of influencers and bloggers who have a similar audience as your target market that you could reach out to for collaborating. You can even include other shop owners who sell different products but to the same market.

2020 GOAL SETTING

CONVERSION RATE

You can also increase your conversion rate by making your site more sales-friendly. There may be things going on in your shop that are inadvertently turning off potential buyers.

Take a close look at your shop and see where potential buyers may be getting hung up. Brainstorm a few ways in the box below to make your shop more sales-friendly. Here are some examples:

- Clarifying confusing product listing descriptions or pricing

- Replacing negative reviews with more positive ones

- Providing easy access to answers to FAQs so a buyer doesn't have to ask

- Simplifying the checkout process

- Clearly stating shipping and refund policies

- Using more professional, clear, and bright product photos

- Making your categories and shop set up easy for browsing and searching within your shop

It's always fun to grab a few volunteers and ask them to "browse out loud" in your shop. This may lead to a few conversion-boosting fixes you would never have thought of on your own.

2020 GOAL SETTING

PRODUCTS

TAKE-HOME PAY GOAL → NET INCOME GOAL → SALES GOAL & EXPENSE GOAL → ORDERS GOAL → PRODUCTS & PRODUCT MIX

You now know about how many orders you need to get to achieve your sales goal, and how much traffic you need to drive to your shop to get those orders. But what will you sell to these visitors? What will they order?

The next few exercises will help you narrow down where to focus your energy to best achieve your goals. We want to work efficiently and effectively, and your time is best spent on the products that are **profitable**, which could mean various things to you.

A profitable product may be the item that sells best in your shop. Your bestselling product is the one that you sell over and over again that generates the most orders for you or maybe even the most in *sales dollars*.

However, your bestselling product may not necessarily your most *profitable* product - because profit is truly defined as sales minus expenses. That means the retail price of the product minus the cost of creating it.

If your bestselling item sells for $10 and costs you $6 to make, that item is contributing $4 towards your net income (it's got a 40% profit margin). You might have another product that sells for $8 but only costs you $3 to make. This product contributes $5 to your net income (it's got a 50% profit margin). It may be better for you to focus more time and energy on marketing the item with a better profit margin, even though it has a lower selling price.

This exercise is not meant to be totally black & white. Sometimes it works to have a best-selling item with a "bad" or lower profit margin. If you're selling enough of them, you can still totally meet your goals. **My purpose is to bring your attention to the profitability of your popular products and see that different items will help reach your goals faster or slower, depending on their profitability**. Remember, we're all about working smarter, not harder!

2020 GOAL SETTING

PRODUCTS

If you sell unique, one-of-a-kind creations, you may find this set of exercises less helpful. It works best for those who create similar products over and over again, or at least similar versions of the same product type. If you are able to think of your unique products in broader categories with general costs or prices, you can still benefit from working through these numbers.

Before we drill down to your specific products or categories, we will forecast your product mix. Do not focus too much on figuring out exactly how much of each type of product type you will sell in 2020. Product mix is quite a volatile number for us to predict with any sort of reliability. The important thing as a seller is that you are selling something and that something is profitable for you. Trends or ebbs & flows in your product line are normal and expected.

That being said, using last year's results, you can forecast about how many of each product type you will sell in 2020 to meet your orders goal. **I encourage you to use this forecast more for budgeting and planning purposes** - like how much supplies & raw materials to order or keep in stock to reach your sales levels goals - rather than as a measuring stick for whether you're reaching those goals.

The important thing is to make sure that whatever you are selling, you're truly making a profit on each sale so that you can pay yourself.

2020 GOAL SETTING

PRODUCT MIX

Review last year's product sales from page 13 of this workbook. Multiply each of these same sales percentages by your total orders goal for 2020 from page 47 to get your predicted number of items sold for each product category.

	PRODUCTS OR CATEGORIES	% OF TOTAL SALES IN 2019	FORECAST OF ITEMS SOLD IN 2020 *Apply % to orders goal*
1			
2			
3			
4			
5			
6			
7			
8			
9			
10			
	ALL OTHER PRODUCTS		

2020 GOAL SETTING

PRODUCTS

Now let's take a moment to walk through some of your most popular items and review their profit margin, keeping in mind how many you anticipate selling in 2020 in order to reach your overall sales & order goals.

Beginning on the next page, you will find 8 product cards where you can figure out the profit margin on your bestselling products, along with how much sales that product could contribute to your bottom line, based on the product mix exercise you just did.

I encourage you to let this new understanding change the way you price or market your goods. Maybe it's time to raise the price on your bestseller. Or maybe it's time to shift your main marketing efforts to another product. Or maybe you can develop a new version of your bestselling product that costs less to create.

Brainstorm some ways to capitalize on these insights below.

2020 GOAL SETTING

PRODUCTS

Product Name:

SALES PRICE	
COST OF GOODS (raw materials & supplies):	
PROFIT (sales price - cost):	
How many do I anticipate selling in 2020?	
How much does that contribute to my sales? (number sold x sales price)	
How much does that contribute to my net income? (number sold x profit)	

Product Name:

SALES PRICE	
COST OF GOODS (raw materials & supplies):	
PROFIT (sales price - cost):	
How many do I anticipate selling in 2020?	
How much does that contribute to my sales? (number sold x sales price)	
How much does that contribute to my net income? (number sold x profit)	

2020 GOAL SETTING

PRODUCTS

Product Name:

SALES PRICE	
COST OF GOODS (raw materials & supplies):	
PROFIT (sales price - cost):	
How many do I anticipate selling in 2020?	
How much does that contribute to my sales? (number sold x sales price)	
How much does that contribute to my net income? (number sold x profit)	

Product Name:

SALES PRICE	
COST OF GOODS (raw materials & supplies):	
PROFIT (sales price - cost):	
How many do I anticipate selling in 2020?	
How much does that contribute to my sales? (number sold x sales price)	
How much does that contribute to my net income? (number sold x profit)	

2020 GOAL SETTING

PRODUCTS

Product Name:

SALES PRICE	
COST OF GOODS (raw materials & supplies):	
PROFIT (sales price - cost):	
How many do I anticipate selling in 2020?	
How much does that contribute to my sales? (number sold x sales price)	
How much does that contribute to my net income? (number sold x profit)	

Product Name:

SALES PRICE	
COST OF GOODS (raw materials & supplies):	
PROFIT (sales price - cost):	
How many do I anticipate selling in 2020?	
How much does that contribute to my sales? (number sold x sales price)	
How much does that contribute to my net income? (number sold x profit)	

2020 GOAL SETTING

PRODUCTS

Product Name:

SALES PRICE	
COST OF GOODS (raw materials & supplies):	
PROFIT (sales price - cost):	
How many do I anticipate selling in 2020?	
How much does that contribute to my sales? (number sold x sales price)	
How much does that contribute to my net income? (number sold x profit)	

Product Name:

SALES PRICE	
COST OF GOODS (raw materials & supplies):	
PROFIT (sales price - cost):	
How many do I anticipate selling in 2020?	
How much does that contribute to my sales? (number sold x sales price)	
How much does that contribute to my net income? (number sold x profit)	

2020 GOAL SETTING

EXPENSES

TAKE-HOME PAY GOAL → NET INCOME GOAL → SALES GOAL & EXPENSE GOAL → SPENDING BUDGET

Back on page 46, we worked backwards from your net income goal to set both your sales AND your expense goal. We've ignored the expenses part of that equation until now.

TOTAL 2020 EXPENSES (FROM PREVIOUS EXERCISE) $

You calculated an annual amount for expenses based on your prior year profit margin ratio. I want you to take a hard look at this expense amount and see if it seems reasonable. Remember, this number is really just a vague estimate based on last year's results. We're saying that however we spent money in relation to how much we made in sales last year will be very similar to how we will do so this year.

You might already know that 2020 is likely going to be different - you may plan to invest in a new piece of equipment in 2020, or you may not have a bunch of start up costs from last year again. So adjust this number if necessary. If you change your total expenses, keep in mind that changes your total net income too. Every number is part of a constantly moving puzzle!

Once you have a total expense estimate in mind (whether you decide to keep the one you previously calculated or tweak it a bit), I want you to turn this number into your business' budget for 2020. That's right, I said the dirty b word - budget.

We will break this total expense down into your expense categories. This might feel like taking a stab in the dark unless you have prior year data to compare it to. If you don't, that's totally fine. Just do the best you can as always!

MY TOTAL 2020 BUDGET FOR SPENDING $

2020 GOAL SETTING

EXPENSES

On the chart below, take your total spending budget and break it down by expense category, just like you did with the 2019 table. Re-write the percentages you previously calculated for 2019 on page 16, and apply those to the total spending budget for 2020. This will give you an estimated breakdown of how much you can expect to spend on those categories in 2020.

ESTIMATED SPENDING BASED ON LAST YEAR'S RESULTS		
EXPENSE BREAKDOWN	% OF TOTAL SPENDING IN 2019	TOTAL AMOUNT BUDGETED FOR 2020
RAW MATERIALS & SUPPLIES		
ETSY FEES, PAYPAL FEES, ETC.		
SHIPPING & PACKAGING		
ADVERTISING		
APPS & SOFTWARE		
OFFICE EXPENSES		
PROFESSIONAL SERVICES		
EDUCATION & TRAINING		
Total Spending in 2020 =		

2020 BUDGETING - EXPENSES

Before moving too far forward with the total expense budget you just set, let's take a look at your predicted recurring fixed monthly & annual expenses. A lot of business expenses are variable, like how much you may spend on supplies, advertising, education, etc. But you likely have a lot of rather predictable fixed expenses, and some of these are often monthly.

Here are some ideas of what expenses to look out for:

- Email subscription service
- Social media schedulers
- Web domain fees
- Virtual assistant or contractor fees
- G-suite
- Creative Cloud or software subscriptions
- Monthly memberships
- Recurring fixed sales platform fees

Take a look at your last few months of expenses and jot down your predictable recurring monthly or annual expenses in the box on the next page. Most will likely be monthly, but you may have a few annual expenses that happen once each year as well. Take time to crawl through last year's books to find this info and predict as accurately as possible.

After compiling this info, now is a great time to cut back on any of these recurring monthly fees you no longer need. Build more room in your budget or increase your profit margin!

Next, you want to make sure you have enough room in your budget for the total of these fixed recurring fees, plus all your other expenses that month.

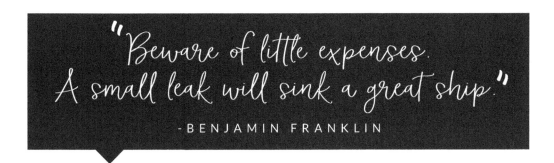

"Beware of little expenses. A small leak will sink a great ship."

-BENJAMIN FRANKLIN

2020 GOAL SETTING

EXPENSES

MONTHLY FIXED EXPENSES	AMOUNT
TOTAL MONTHLY FIXED EXPENSES =	
x12 =	

ANNUAL FIXED EXPENSES	AMOUNT
TOTAL ANNUAL FIXED EXPENSES =	

2020 GOAL SETTING

EXPENSES

Does your new budget seem reasonable to you? It is likely you may want to make adjustments here, so I'm leaving you with a new blank table below if you want to re-work anything or use adjusted percentages for 2020.

A few thoughts - If you have increased sales to meet your 2020 goals, you will likely need to spend more than previous years on raw materials & supplies to meet that demand. You may also spend more on things like Etsy fees, advertising, etc. However, you might not necessarily need to increase your budget for more "fixed" costs like your website fees, your office expenses, or your education & training. So tweak these estimates now to meet your projections for 2020.

ESTIMATED SPENDING FOR 2020		
EXPENSE BREAKDOWN	ESTIMATED % OF SPENDING IN 2020	TOTAL AMOUNT BUDGETED FOR 2020
RAW MATERIALS & SUPPLIES		
ETSY FEES, PAYPAL FEES, ETC.		
SHIPPING & PACKAGING		
ADVERTISING		
APPS & SOFTWARE		
OFFICE EXPENSES		
PROFESSIONAL SERVICES		
EDUCATION & TRAINING		
Total Spending in 2020 =		

2020 GOAL SETTING

SOCIAL MEDIA

One of the ways you can reach your financial goals is to grow your audience. Different audiences may be more or less important to you, depending on what works for your business. Let's set some number goals for your social media outlets and other venues below. Feel free to skip any rows that are not important to you.

	NUMBER GOALS TO ACHIEVE BY THE END OF 2020
FACEBOOK PAGE FANS	
FB POSTS PER WEEK	
FACEBOOK GROUP MEMBERS	
INSTAGRAM FOLLOWERS	
IG POSTS PER WEEK	
TWITTER FOLLOWERS	
YOUTUBE FOLLOWERS	
VIDEO UPLOADS PER MONTH	
PINTEREST FOLLOWERS	
SNAPCHAT FOLLOWERS	
EMAIL SUBSCRIBERS	
E-NEWSLETTERS PER MONTH	
BLOG SUBSCRIBERS	
BLOG POSTS PER MONTH	

2020 GOAL SETTING

BREAK IT DOWN

Before we brainstorm how we use our time, we can break down our goals into monthly increments to make them a bit more approachable. Use the chart on pages 71-72 to break down your big annual goals into monthly amounts by sales, number of orders, expenses, net income (which will just be your sales minus expenses), and visitors.

HOW TO BREAK DOWN YOUR ANNUAL GOALS TO MONTHLY GOALS:

1. Divvy up your sales goal (keeping in mind the tips below).

2. Divvy up your number of orders goal, based on the sales goal for that month. *Use your average sales dollar per order if needed.*

3. Divvy up your number of visitors goal, based on the orders goal for that month. *Use your conversion rate stat from last year if needed.*

4. Divvy up your expense budget, keeping your sales goal in mind.

5. Calculate the month's net income goal by subtracting your expense goal from your sales goal.

A FEW THINGS TO KEEP IN MIND AS YOU BREAK IT DOWN:

- Time of year affects your sales. Don't let this exercise be as literal as taking your annual goal and dividing it by 12. I want you to also consider how the time of year affects your sales. There's a brief overview of 2020 holidays to think about on the next page.

- Your expenses will usually coordinate with your sales. When sales increase, expenses likely increase somewhat, and vice versa. Think about this as you divvy up that expense budget throughout the year.

- Make sure that the total of all months matches the annual goals you set on the previous pages. You can use the area below the chart on page 72 to make sure all your totals match.

2020 GOAL SETTING

BREAK IT DOWN

- It may help you to see us work through the break down process visually and live in the Goal-Getting Facebook group.

- As you break out your annual goals by month, you may decide to adjust your total overall goals, which is fine. Seeing it on a monthly basis may cause you to think *Gee, I know I can do better than that in this month*. Or alternatively, you might think something like *There's no way I can make that amount in a month!* So if you need to make adjustments to the overall totals, that's totally fine.

In the handmade industry, we deal with a lot of highs and lows based on the season. Holiday sales are going strong in November and December, while summer can be really slow. I've got a short list of holidays & events that might affect your sales below. Keep these in mind as you set sales goals for each month.

2020 US HOLIDAYS & EVENTS

- **January** - New Year's, Martin Luther King Day
- **February** - Valentine's Day, President's Day weekend, Mardi Gras, Lenten Season Starts
- **March** - St. Patrick's Day, Lenten season begins
- **April** - Lenten Season Ends, Easter, Passover, Earth Day
- **May** - Cinco de Mayo, Mother's Day, Memorial Day weekend
- **June** - Father's Day

- **July** - Independence Day
- **August** - Back To School
- **September** - Back To School, Labor Day weekend, Rosh Hashana, Grandparent's Day
- **October** - Halloween
- **November** - Veteran's Day, Thanksgiving, Black Friday, Cyber Monday
- **December** - Christmas, Hanukkah, Kwanzaa, New Year's Eve

2020 GOAL SETTING

BREAK IT DOWN

January	February	March
SALES:	SALES:	SALES:
NO. OF ORDERS:	NO. OF ORDERS:	NO. OF ORDERS:
VISITORS:	VISITORS:	VISITORS:
EXPENSES:	EXPENSES:	EXPENSES:
NET:	NET:	NET:
April	May	June
SALES:	SALES:	SALES:
NO. OF ORDERS:	NO. OF ORDERS:	NO. OF ORDERS:
VISITORS:	VISITORS:	VISITORS:
EXPENSES:	EXPENSES:	EXPENSES:
NET:	NET:	NET:

2020 GOAL SETTING

BREAK IT DOWN

July	August	September
SALES:	SALES:	SALES:
NO. OF ORDERS:	NO. OF ORDERS:	NO. OF ORDERS:
VISITORS:	VISITORS:	VISITORS:
EXPENSES:	EXPENSES:	EXPENSES:
NET:	NET:	NET:
October	November	December
SALES:	SALES:	SALES:
NO. OF ORDERS:	NO. OF ORDERS:	NO. OF ORDERS:
VISITORS:	VISITORS:	VISITORS:
EXPENSES:	EXPENSES:	EXPENSES:
NET:	NET:	NET:

2020 SALES GOAL $ 2020 EXPENSE GOAL $

2020 ORDERS GOAL   2020 NET INCOME GOAL $

2020 GOAL SETTING

BREAK IT DOWN

☑ **TAKE-HOME PAY GOAL:** _____

☑ **NET INCOME GOAL:** _____

☑ **SALES GOAL:** _____

☑ **EXPENSE GOAL & BUDGET:** _____

☑ **NUMBER OF ORDERS GOAL:** _____

☑ **TRAFFIC/NUMBER OF VISITORS GOAL :** _____

☑ **PRODUCT & PRODUCT MIX GOAL:** _____

Look how far you've come my friend! You've set some HUGE goals for 2020. You now know a lot of stuff, like how many orders you need to fill to reach your sales goals and what products to focus your energy on to achieve these goals. You even know the milestones you need to hit each month to meet these goals.

Now comes the important part - **planning out your time** so you can take real action steps to achieve those goals.

What do you actually need to **do** to achieve these things each month? Hopefully as you've worked throughout our previous exercises in Parts 1 & 2, you've come up with a few golden nuggets on how to build traffic, traction and sales in your business. We're going to work through a few more exercises that help us whittle your big goals down to actionable daily tasks.

There is absolutely no point in crunching all these numbers and setting goals if you do not allow these goals to dictate the way you run your business. Picture your goals (or more specifically, that big dreamy take-home pay goal - remember that guy?!) as the destination on your map. Now we're going to create the route to get you there.

Meet Your New Boss - Your Goals.

2020 GOAL SETTING

BRAINSTORMING

Let's do a little general brainstorming here, then focus our ideas into a defined actionable strategy next.

Based on my previous experience, what can I do in 2020 to help me achieve my goals? If you're looking for ideas, these might be things like host giveaways, use brand reps, focus your social media time on Instagram vs. Pinterest, do a specific local craft show again, etc. Look at what worked well in 2020 and replicate it.

What new things do I want to try in 2020? Ideas might be a new craft show or event, blogging, outsourcing Pinterest to a virtual assistant, promoting listings on Etsy, advertising in a local magazine, collaborating with a specific influencer, etc.

2020 GOAL SETTING

BRAINSTORMING

Product development and creation may be an important way to reach your financial goals in 2020. You may want to set goals to create a new product line every quarter, or release 2 new designs each month. Jot down any goals specific to product creation here, and make sure to be specific about the timing. It's not good enough to say that you want to release a holiday line. You need to have it done by a certain date in order to fully capitalize on that holiday traffic! Give yourself a deadline. It's not enough to say I want to develop 8 new products this year; make it 2 new products every quarter.

We are focused on taking action, so be specific. Examples:

- 100 products listed in my shop before Mother's Day 2020
- 3 new product lines by year end, one released for Spring (April 1), one released for Summer (July 1), and one for the holiday season (October 15)
- 10 new notebook designs listed in time for back-to-school shoppers, by July 20
- A holiday card line listed by November 1

WHAT QUANTIFIABLE PRODUCT-RELATED GOALS OR MILESTONES DO I HAVE FOR 2020?

2020 GOAL SETTING

FOCUS

You've done your financial goal-setting work, and you've also spent some time brainstorming some strategies. We're going to break down all these plans to **qualitative goals** that I like to call focus points.

You have also broken down your financial numbers month by month. We will break down your **qualitative** goals for each month of 2020 as well.

Throughout the goal-setting exercises we've done for 2020, certain concepts or key components may have surfaced as weaker points in your business. There were likely a handful of key areas, or **focus points**, that need to be improved upon in order to meet your financial take-home pay goal.

Circle the key focus points you need to work on for 2020 (the first few are from Part 2 exercises that may have exposed specific weaknesses in your business, the next are just common focus point ideas). Write in any others that you have come up with on your own.

I don't want you to have any more than 12. Too many things to juggle means doing no one thing well.

Remember, these focus points are BROAD areas of improvement that can be broken down into more action steps. For example, increasing traffic to your site can entail guest posting, email marketing, social media outreach, improving SEO, etc. Next, we will brainstorm action points to work on these.

FOCUS POINTS

Circle the key focus points you need to work on for 2020. Use the blank spaces to write in any others that you have come up with.

- INCREASING PROFITABILITY AND PROFIT MARGIN
- INCREASING AVERAGE DOLLAR AMOUNT PER ORDER
- IMPROVE CONVERSION RATES
- IMPROVING SPECIFIC SKILL

- BUILDING NEW SITE OR EXPLORING NEW SALES VENUE
- DEVELOPING NEW OR IMPROVED PRODUCTS
- INCREASE TRAFFIC TO SITE
-

-
-
-
-

2020 GOAL SETTING

FOCUS

Remember that chart of 2019 KPIs you summarized back on page 27? As we set focus points and plan actions steps for 2020, let's revisit the ones you marked as needing improvement. Here are a few ideas for how to improve your stats that you may want to work into your plan for the year.

STATISTIC	IMPROVEMENT IDEAS
PROFIT MARGIN PERCENTAGE	Analyze pricing strategy for long-term profitability. Increase pricing and/or decrease cost of goods sold. Decrease spending or cut unnecessary expenses. Increase sales (increase traffic, products offered, conversion rate, etc.).
AVERAGE SALE AMOUNT PER ORDER AVERAGE ITEMS SOLD PER ORDER	Increase pricing. Bundle products or offer gift sets. Link to related or complimentary products throughout shop. More ideas discussed on pages 48-49.
VIEWS TO VISITORS RATIO BOUNCE RATE AVERAGE TIME ON PAGE	Keep visitors on your page longer and shopping within your site longer. Clearly state answers to FAQs, shipping policies, refund policy, etc. in accessible place or within listings. Clear professional photographs, copywriting, and branding. Links to related listings, policies, etc. as needed. Minimal ads or links to outside sites.
CONVERSION RATE	All of the above apply! Also, remove anything that makes checkout time-consuming or confusing. Focus on marketing tactics that attract your ideal customer to your shop, not just anybody. Craft copy that speaks to your ideal customer specifically. See more info on improving your conversion rate on pages 53-54.

2020 GOAL SETTING

FOCUS

Do the focus points you just chose on page 76 also help you improve the stats you selected as needing improvement from last year? If not, you may need to add one or two to your box on page 76.

Focus points for the year

Let's divvy up your focus points to each month of the year, just like we did with your financial goals.

A FEW THINGS TO KEEP IN MIND AS YOU BREAK IT DOWN:

- Keep in mind the sales, orders, and visitors goals you set each month back on pages 71-72. Your focus points should correspond to these. For example, if you have a focus point to develop a new holiday product line, you will want to assign that focus point to a month that allows you the time to release the new products before the holiday season.

- Some focus points have a snowball effect, and I encourage you to assign those to the beginning of the year to make them most effective. Strategies to increase traffic can help you build your number of visitors throughout the entire year. Focusing on that in January will reap rewards throughout the year. Which focus points will benefit you the most by doing them sooner vs later?

- I'd strive for one focus point per month so you don't get overwhelmed, but this depends on how much time and energy you have to devote to your business AND the weight of the specific focus point.

- Some focus points may be so involved that you need to dedicate multiple months to them, and that's okay. There's no right or wrong here. You could even think of them as quarterly focus points instead.

2020 GOAL SETTING

FOCUS POINTS FOR THE YEAR

January	February	March	April
FOCUS:	FOCUS:	FOCUS:	FOCUS:

May	June	July	August
FOCUS:	FOCUS:	FOCUS:	FOCUS:

September	October	November	December
FOCUS: Weddings	FOCUS:	FOCUS:	FOCUS:

2020 GOAL SETTING

FOCUS POINTS FOR THE YEAR

Now we will take each focus point and break it down into the related tactics, strategies, and daily actions. These tactics and actions will help you create a day-to-day plan of attack within each month. **We are striving to run your business in a way where each and every day you are doing at least one thing to move a tiny step closer to your goal.**

If it helps, you can initially brain dump all the possible actions or strategies you could pursue regarding this focus point. After your initial brain dump, I want you to look at your list in light of what you know has worked well and not worked well for your business in the past. Scratch out anything that you feel is a waste of energy or just not a good fit. Time is a precious resource here, so get honest with yourself and get focused.

Finally, I want you to remind yourself of any specific concrete goals you set regarding this focus point in a previous exercise. So if your focus point was to increase traffic, and your visitors goal for the year was to get 31,000 visitors in your shop, you'd write that specific visitors goal in the bottom box.

Focus Point:

ACTIONS & STRATEGIES TO PURSUE:

2020 GOAL:

2020 GOAL SETTING

FOCUS POINTS FOR THE YEAR

Focus Point:

ACTIONS & STRATEGIES TO PURSUE:

2020 GOAL:

Focus Point:

ACTIONS & STRATEGIES TO PURSUE:

2020 GOAL:

2020 GOAL SETTING

FOCUS POINTS FOR THE YEAR

Focus Point:

ACTIONS & STRATEGIES TO PURSUE:

2020 GOAL:

Focus Point:

ACTIONS & STRATEGIES TO PURSUE:

2020 GOAL:

2020 GOAL SETTING

FOCUS POINTS FOR THE YEAR

Focus Point:

ACTIONS & STRATEGIES TO PURSUE:

2020 GOAL:

Focus Point:

ACTIONS & STRATEGIES TO PURSUE:

2020 GOAL:

2020 GOAL SETTING

FOCUS POINTS FOR THE YEAR

Focus Point:

ACTIONS & STRATEGIES TO PURSUE:

2020 GOAL:

Focus Point:

ACTIONS & STRATEGIES TO PURSUE:

2020 GOAL:

2020 GOAL SETTING

FOCUS POINTS FOR THE YEAR

Focus Point:

ACTIONS & STRATEGIES TO PURSUE:

2020 GOAL:

Focus Point:

ACTIONS & STRATEGIES TO PURSUE:

2020 GOAL:

2020 GOAL SETTING

FOCUS POINTS FOR THE YEAR

Focus Point:

ACTIONS & STRATEGIES TO PURSUE:

2020 GOAL:

Focus Point:

ACTIONS & STRATEGIES TO PURSUE:

2020 GOAL:

2020 GOAL SETTING

PLANNING TO PAY YOURSELF

Since setting the goal to pay yourself is the foundation of all your goal-setting work, I want to revisit that topic one more time. Visualize paying yourself from your business. How does it feel? More importantly, what does the process look like?

I don't want you to think of paying yourself in general terms. Let's plan out some concrete steps to ensure that it happens.

TAKE HOME PAY GOAL:

HOW OFTEN WILL YOU PAY YOURSELF?

HOW WILL YOU PAY YOURSELF?
(write a check, withdraw cash, electronic transfer, etc.)

HOW WILL YOU CALCULATE HOW MUCH TO PAY YOURSELF EACH PERIOD?
(set percentage of sales, specific amount each time, any amount over $X, etc.)

As you set your parameters around your plan to pay yourself, make sure it fits in with your overall goal amount.

2020 GOAL SETTING

PLANNING TO PAY YOURSELF

METHODS OF PAYING YOURSELF

Assuming you are a sole proprietor, there are several different methods of deciding how much to pay yourself from your business. Here are just a few:

- A determined fixed amount each week/month (ex: $1000 a month)

- Any amount over a specific threshold left in the bank account each month (ex: any amount over $5000 in my bank account on the first of each month)

- A set percentage of net income from your business each month (ex: 25% of my net income each month, so if in January I made $5400 in net income - sales minus expenses - then I will pay myself $1350)

- A set percentage of sales each month, regardless of expenses (ex: 25% of my sales each month, so if in January I grossed $7000 in sales, then I will pay myself $1750)

None of these methods are the "most right". The perk of running your own business is that YOU get to choose. I just strongly encourage you to choose some method, because paying yourself something (rather than nothing) is very important to creating a sustainable and *fulfilling business*.

I personally prefer the last bullet point method above — paying yourself based on a percentage of sales. This encourages you to run a leaner business and follows the frequently mentioned "Profit First" payment model (based on the popular book *Profit First* by Mike Michalowicz.

Paying yourself based on a percentage of **gross sales**, before taking any expenses into account, means you will ALWAYS pay yourself something (as long as you have sales that month). Your expenses are paid AFTER paying yourself, so you prevent yourself from running at a loss or not paying yourself because you spent too much on expenses. That's why this method encourages you to run a leaner, more cost-efficient business.

You certainly don't have to embrace this method, but I encourage you to try it out for a few months. You can start with whatever percentage you feel comfortable with — there's no right or wrong number. Get in the habit of transferring this amount every week or month to your personal account and see how good it feels to get paid from your hard work!

2020 GOAL SETTING

PLANNING TO PAY YOURSELF

I WILL PAY MYSELF

☐ —————— % OF NET INCOME

☐ —————— % OF SALES

☐ A FIXED AMOUNT OF $—————

☐ ANY AMOUNT OVER $ —————— IN MY ACCOUNT

☐ AT THIS FREQUENCY—————————————————

Now check in with how your set plan lines up with your overall take-home pay goal for the year. The frequency multiplied by the amounts needs to get you somewhere around that total annual goal. If it doesn't seem feasible, you may need to make some adjustments to your plan!

> "A financially healthy company is a result of a series of daily financial wins, not one big moment. Profitability isn't an event, it's a habit."
>
> -MIKE MICHALOWICZ

2020 GOAL SETTING

GUIDE MAP

Ready to bring it ALL together? This may be a bit repetitive, but on the next page, I want you to take everything we've covered so far - all the goals we've set - the financial stuff, the qualitative focus points, etc. - and map them out over the year. This one page will serve as your summarized **guide map** throughout the year.

Pin this page on your office wall, tape to your mirror, etc. Put it somewhere where you will see it throughout the year. You will always know at a glance if you are focusing your time, money, and energy on the tasks you set for yourself to reach your goals.

Having your guide map handy will keep you on track. It is so easy to get sidetracked or develop shiny object syndrome throughout the year. The farther we get from when we set our goals, the easier it is for us to forget them. Keep this page visible and reflect on it from time to time, at least quarterly.

Remember - your goal is your boss. Let it guide your day-to-day work. When you're presented with a new opportunity or have a new idea, check in with your goal and your guide map. Does this fit in with your vision?

If it doesn't, it's time to scrap it. Record it wherever you like to "brain dump" your ideas, save it for a rainy day, and move on to the action steps necessary to achieve the goals you have set. If it does fit in, it's likely already on your guide map somewhere!

Remember - your goal is your boss.
Let it guide your day-to-day work.

2020 GOAL SETTING

GUIDE MAP

January	February	March
SALES GOAL:	SALES GOAL:	SALES GOAL:
ORDERS GOAL:	ORDERS GOAL:	ORDERS GOAL:
FOCUS POINTS:	FOCUS POINTS:	FOCUS POINTS:

April	May	June
SALES GOAL:	SALES GOAL:	SALES GOAL:
ORDERS GOAL:	ORDERS GOAL:	ORDERS GOAL:
FOCUS POINTS:	FOCUS POINTS:	FOCUS POINTS:

July	August	September
SALES GOAL:	SALES GOAL:	SALES GOAL:
ORDERS GOAL:	ORDERS GOAL:	ORDERS GOAL:
FOCUS POINTS:	FOCUS POINTS:	FOCUS POINTS:

October	November	December
SALES GOAL:	SALES GOAL:	SALES GOAL:
ORDERS GOAL:	ORDERS GOAL:	ORDERS GOAL:
FOCUS POINTS:	FOCUS POINTS:	FOCUS POINTS:

2020 GOAL SETTING

TIME MANAGEMENT

As creative entrepreneurs who are likely juggling many things in life other than "just" running a business, we can't talk about setting financial goals and focus points without also thinking about time management skills.

The ability to effectively use however much (or little) time you have is likely the #1 factor to whether you will achieve the goals you set in this workbook. It's also the #1 excuse we use to explain why we fail to reach our goals. So let's briefly discuss ways to improve our time management skills, and come up with some parameters to encourage us to use our time wisely this year.

TRACK YOUR TIME.

I encourage you to begin your journey to better time management by simply measuring your available work time. Let's get a baseline - how many hours a week are you currently working on your business?

Use an app or a timer to track your working time for 2-3 weeks. This exercise will make you more aware of the choices you are making and whether you are effectively using the time you do have.

Personally, tracking my time made me realize I spent more time than I would've guessed working on my shop. I had enough hours to get closer to my goals - the fact that I wasn't getting there meant that I wasn't using these hours wisely enough.

The point of time tracking is not necessarily to create more time or expand your work hours into other parts of your day or week (although you may literally just need MORE hours!). It's to shift your focus to quality, not quantity. Sometime re-prioritizing how we are spending these limited hours makes all the difference in our productivity.

IT BOILS DOWN TO CHOICES.

Effective time management and getting things done boils down to your choices. We are ALL limited on time - how are you choosing to use the limited hours you have? If you aren't using your time wisely, it's not time's fault. It's not your family's fault or your day job boss's fault or Netflix's fault - it's your fault.

2020 GOAL SETTING

TIME MANAGEMENT

When you sit down to work, what are you choosing to work on? Revisit our discussion of the three main types of activities in your business from page 33:

- Revenue-generating activities
- Momentum-building activities
- Maintenance activities

Maintenance activities are easy to fall into. We can spend a lot of time crafting social media posts, browsing our Facebook groups, and refreshing our Etsy stats and "feel" busy. But a week of mostly maintenance activities means not getting much real work done, and thus not working towards achieving the goals you have set.

Revenue-generating and momentum-building activities are the things that will truly inch your business closer to your financial goals. This is the work you want to prioritize to spend your time effectively. We want to build in processes and systems to ensure you are spending most of your energy here.

DECIDE HOW YOU WILL SPEND YOUR TIME IN 2020.

We've already done work breaking down your focus points to the action steps you will take in 2020. Now, I encourage you to fill out the next page and write out all the revenue-generating & momentum-building activities you will focus on in the new year. Make sure to include the important action steps you listed for your focus points back on pages 80-87.

Contrast this with the maintenance activities and the "busy work" that you will work on minimizing. Fill out the two boxes on Page 94 and the left-hand box on Page 95, referring back to page 32 if you need examples of activities you did last year.

2020 GOAL SETTING

TIME MANAGEMENT

HOW WILL YOU SPEND YOUR TIME?

Fill out the two boxes below and write out all the revenue-generating & momentum-building activities you will focus on in the new year. Then, fill out the left-hand box on the next page referring back to page 32 if you need examples of activities you did last year.

REVENUE-GENERATING ACTIVITIES

MOMENTUM-BUILDING ACTIVITIES

2020 GOAL SETTING

TIME MANAGEMENT

BUSY WORK / MAINTENANCE ACTIVITIES

BOUNDARIES

CREATE BOUNDARIES AROUND YOUR MAINTENANCE ACTIVITIES.

How can you resist the temptation to spend the bulk of your time on maintenance activities? Create boundaries around your work. How that looks specifically for you may vary on your personality type. Here are some examples:

- Set a timer for answering emails, interacting on social media, or any other activity that feels like a time suck

- Set aside certain days or times of day for dealing with your inbox

- Use a scheduling app for social media or Pinterest so you can set it and forget it without needing to log in or get distracted

- Create a detailed FAQ page and canned responses for responding to customer inquiries

- Outsource a maintenance activity to a contractor or assistant

Creating these boundaries, which are essentially rules, helps you run your business more efficiently and spend your limited time on the work that matters most - the activities that will grow your reach and make you money.

Decide on boundaries that will help you mitigate the time spent on busy work. Write them down next to the corresponding maintenance task in the "Boundaries" box on the previous page.

Need more help?

CHECK OUT MY COURSE ALL ABOUT
TIME MANAGEMENT & PRODUCTIVITY, ASANA FOR MAKERS

Asana for Makers provides a bridge between the goals you set in this guidebook and your day to day activity working in your business.

In the course, I teach you how to use a totally free productivity & project management tool called Asana to break down your goals into daily to do's, set recurring reminders for admin activities, batch schedule your time, and much more. Asana for Makers will help you use your time more effectively to reach your goals faster, WHILE still keeping your sanity.

I share the exact system and mindset shifts I've utilized to set and surpass my annual revenue goals from year to year (even while working from home with two constantly babbling toddlers). The system is sort of like creating your own boss for your business - so when you're feeling frazzled, overwhelmed, or uncertain how to move the needle of your business forward, you can log in and know exactly what work needs to be done that day.

Asana for Makers is one part goal-setting concepts, one part productivity mindset, and one part how-to tutorials on how to use Asana and other automation tools to make your life easier. In this course, you'll learn how to:

- Utilize time-saving hacks especially for online sellers
- Create processes and schedule time for common tasks like order fulfillment, blog content creation, admin tasks, and bookkeeping
- Automatically dump your orders from ALL venues in one place so you can streamline your customer service
- Create an annual & quarterly roadmap for your big goals
- Break down the big goals you set in your Guidebook into actionable day-to-day work
- Build in time for reviewing results, tracking your progress, and evaluating the health of your business

LEARN MORE AT ASANAFORMAKERS.COM

part 3:
2020 PROGRESS

2020 PROGRESS

Track your progress!

The rest of this workbook is designed to help you track your progress throughout the year towards the goals you have set.

Fill each month's tracker out at the end of the month or the beginning of the next month - schedule time & reminder alerts in your calendar now! As you do this, take that month's results and compare it to:

- Your 2020 Goal-Setting chart by month - how did you do compared to the goals you set for this month? (You can compare to your monthly chart on pages 71-72.)

- Your Social Media chart - how close are you to hitting your year-end numbers that you set on page 68?

- Your monthly focus chart - how did you do compared to the goals you set for this month?

There are monthly tracker sheets for you to get an idea of everything that happened this month, and there are also annual trackers that let you easily see how you are (hopefully) growing from month-to-month.

Based on this month's results, what do you need to tweak and what do you need to repeat? Are you still on track to meet your overall goals for the year? If yes, great! If not, where do you need to adjust? It's always a moving target, so don't feel frustrated if things don't go exactly according to plan. Your goal is to make sure **you are doing everything YOU can to achieve the goals you have set!**

There are also quarterly progress sheets at the end of each quarter to help you zoom out and review your "big picture" progress.

2020 PROGRESS

JANUARY

FINANCIAL STAT	GOAL	RESULTS
SALES		
EXPENSES		
NET INCOME/LOSS		
PROFIT MARGIN PERCENTAGE		
NUMBER OF ORDERS		
VISITORS		
CONVERSION RATE		

SOCIAL MEDIA	STAT
FACEBOOK	
INSTAGRAM	
TWITTER	
PINTEREST	
EMAIL	
BLOG	

Why did you meet, exceed, or not meet your goals this month?

Did you pay yourself this month? If so, how much?

$

2020 PROGRESS

JANUARY

Actions taken this month

This month's bestselling products

This month's focus point was:

How good of a job did I do working on this focus point?

○──○──○──○──○──○──○──○──○──○
1   2   3   4   5   6   7   8   9   10
☹   ☺

This month's biggest wins

How good of a job did I do keeping boundaries around my busy work?

○──○──○──○──○──○──○──○──○──○
1   2   3   4   5   6   7   8   9   10
☹   ☺

How do I feel about how I performed this month, both from a financial and productivity standpoint?

○──○──○──○──○──○──○──○──○──○
1   2   3   4   5   6   7   8   9   10
☹   ☺

This month's hardest lessons learned

What can I improve next month?

2020 PROGRESS

FEBRUARY

FINANCIAL STAT	GOAL	RESULTS
SALES		
EXPENSES		
NET INCOME/LOSS		
PROFIT MARGIN PERCENTAGE		
NUMBER OF ORDERS		
VISITORS		
CONVERSION RATE		

SOCIAL MEDIA	STAT
FACEBOOK	
INSTAGRAM	
TWITTER	
PINTEREST	
EMAIL	
BLOG	

Why did you meet, exceed, or not meet your goals this month?

Did you pay yourself this month? If so, how much?

$

© JANET LEBLANC, PAPERANDSPARK.COM

2020 PROGRESS

FEBRUARY

Actions taken this month

This month's bestselling products

This month's focus point was:

How good of a job did I do working on this focus point?

1   2   3   4   5   6   7   8   9   10
☹   ☺

This month's biggest wins

How good of a job did I do keeping boundaries around my busy work?

1   2   3   4   5   6   7   8   9   10
☹   ☺

How do I feel about how I performed this month, both from a financial and productivity standpoint?

1   2   3   4   5   6   7   8   9   10
☹   ☺

This month's hardest lessons learned

What can I improve next month?

2020 PROGRESS

MARCH

FINANCIAL STAT	GOAL	RESULTS
SALES		
EXPENSES		
NET INCOME/LOSS		
PROFIT MARGIN PERCENTAGE		
NUMBER OF ORDERS		
VISITORS		
CONVERSION RATE		

SOCIAL MEDIA	STAT
FACEBOOK	
INSTAGRAM	
TWITTER	
PINTEREST	
EMAIL	
BLOG	

Why did you meet, exceed, or not meet your goals this month?

Did you pay yourself this month? If so, how much?

$

2020 PROGRESS

MARCH

Actions taken this month

This month's bestselling products

This month's focus point was:

How good of a job did I do working on this focus point?

1 2 3 4 5 6 7 8 9 10

This month's biggest wins

How good of a job did I do keeping boundaries around my busy work?

1 2 3 4 5 6 7 8 9 10

How do I feel about how I performed this month, both from a financial and productivity standpoint?

1 2 3 4 5 6 7 8 9 10

This month's hardest lessons learned

What can I improve next month?

2020 PROGRESS

QUARTERLY PLANNING

FINANCIAL STAT	GOAL QUARTERLY TOTAL	ACTUAL QUARTERLY TOTAL	NEED TO ADJUST ANNUAL GOAL?
SALES			
EXPENSES			
NET INCOME/LOSS			
PROFIT MARGIN PERCENTAGE			
NUMBER OF ORDERS			
VISITORS			
CONVERSION RATE			

Did you work on your focus points or did you get distracted with shiny objects?

Which strategies have seemed worth your time & energy and which have not?

2020 PROGRESS

QUARTERLY PLANNING

Patterns or trends I've noticed this quarter:

Financial Goals -
What do I need to adjust or change up next quarter?

Focus Points -
What do I need to adjust or change up next quarter?

2020 PROGRESS

APRIL

FINANCIAL STAT	GOAL	RESULTS
SALES		
EXPENSES		
NET INCOME/LOSS		
PROFIT MARGIN PERCENTAGE		
NUMBER OF ORDERS		
VISITORS		
CONVERSION RATE		

SOCIAL MEDIA	STAT
FACEBOOK	
INSTAGRAM	
TWITTER	
PINTEREST	
EMAIL	
BLOG	

Why did you meet, exceed, or not meet your goals this month?

Did you pay yourself this month? If so, how much?

$

2020 PROGRESS

APRIL

Actions taken this month

This month's bestselling products

This month's focus point was:

How good of a job did I do working on this focus point?

1　2　3　4　5　6　7　8　9　10
☹　　　　　　　　　　　　☺

This month's biggest wins

How good of a job did I do keeping boundaries around my busy work?

1　2　3　4　5　6　7　8　9　10
☹　　　　　　　　　　　　☺

How do I feel about how I performed this month, both from a financial and productivity standpoint?

1　2　3　4　5　6　7　8　9　10
☹　　　　　　　　　　　　☺

This month's hardest lessons learned

What can I improve next month?

2020 PROGRESS

MAY

FINANCIAL STAT	GOAL	RESULTS
SALES		
EXPENSES		
NET INCOME/LOSS		
PROFIT MARGIN PERCENTAGE		
NUMBER OF ORDERS		
VISITORS		
CONVERSION RATE		

SOCIAL MEDIA	STAT
FACEBOOK	
INSTAGRAM	
TWITTER	
PINTEREST	
EMAIL	
BLOG	

Why did you meet, exceed, or not meet your goals this month?

Did you pay yourself this month? If so, how much?

$

2020 PROGRESS

MAY

Actions taken this month

This month's bestselling products

This month's focus point was:

How good of a job did I do working on this focus point?

1 2 3 4 5 6 7 8 9 10

This month's biggest wins

How good of a job did I do keeping boundaries around my busy work?

1 2 3 4 5 6 7 8 9 10

How do I feel about how I performed this month, both from a financial and productivity standpoint?

1 2 3 4 5 6 7 8 9 10

This month's hardest lessons learned

What can I improve next month?

2020 PROGRESS

JUNE

FINANCIAL STAT	GOAL	RESULTS
SALES		
EXPENSES		
NET INCOME/LOSS		
PROFIT MARGIN PERCENTAGE		
NUMBER OF ORDERS		
VISITORS		
CONVERSION RATE		

SOCIAL MEDIA	STAT
FACEBOOK	
INSTAGRAM	
TWITTER	
PINTEREST	
EMAIL	
BLOG	

Why did you meet, exceed, or not meet your goals this month?

Did you pay yourself this month? If so, how much?

$

2020 PROGRESS

JUNE

Actions taken this month

This month's bestselling products

This month's focus point was:

How good of a job did I do working on this focus point?

1 2 3 4 5 6 7 8 9 10

This month's biggest wins

How good of a job did I do keeping boundaries around my busy work?

1 2 3 4 5 6 7 8 9 10

How do I feel about how I performed this month, both from a financial and productivity standpoint?

1 2 3 4 5 6 7 8 9 10

This month's hardest lessons learned

What can I improve next month?

2020 PROGRESS

QUARTERLY PLANNING

FINANCIAL STAT	GOAL QUARTERLY TOTAL	ACTUAL QUARTERLY TOTAL	NEED TO ADJUST ANNUAL GOAL?
SALES			
EXPENSES			
NET INCOME/LOSS			
PROFIT MARGIN PERCENTAGE			
NUMBER OF ORDERS			
VISITORS			
CONVERSION RATE			

Did you work on your focus points or did you get distracted with shiny objects?

Which strategies have seemed worth your time & energy and which have not?

2020 PROGRESS

QUARTERLY PLANNING

Patterns or trends I've noticed this quarter:

Financial Goals -
What do I need to adjust or change up next quarter?

Focus Points -
What do I need to adjust or change up next quarter?

2020 PROGRESS

JULY

FINANCIAL STAT	GOAL	RESULTS
SALES		
EXPENSES		
NET INCOME/LOSS		
PROFIT MARGIN PERCENTAGE		
NUMBER OF ORDERS		
VISITORS		
CONVERSION RATE		

SOCIAL MEDIA	STAT
FACEBOOK	
INSTAGRAM	
TWITTER	
PINTEREST	
EMAIL	
BLOG	

Why did you meet, exceed, or not meet your goals this month?

Did you pay yourself this month? If so, how much?

$

© JANET LEBLANC, PAPERANDSPARK.COM

2020 PROGRESS

JULY

Actions taken this month

This month's bestselling products

This month's focus point was:

How good of a job did I do working on this focus point?

1 2 3 4 5 6 7 8 9 10

This month's biggest wins

How good of a job did I do keeping boundaries around my busy work?

1 2 3 4 5 6 7 8 9 10

How do I feel about how I performed this month, both from a financial and productivity standpoint?

1 2 3 4 5 6 7 8 9 10

This month's hardest lessons learned

What can I improve next month?

2020 PROGRESS

AUGUST

FINANCIAL STAT	GOAL	RESULTS
SALES		
EXPENSES		
NET INCOME/LOSS		
PROFIT MARGIN PERCENTAGE		
NUMBER OF ORDERS		
VISITORS		
CONVERSION RATE		

SOCIAL MEDIA	STAT
FACEBOOK	
INSTAGRAM	
TWITTER	
PINTEREST	
EMAIL	
BLOG	

Why did you meet, exceed, or not meet your goals this month?

Did you pay yourself this month? If so, how much?

$

2020 PROGRESS

AUGUST

Actions taken this month

This month's bestselling products

This month's focus point was:

How good of a job did I do working on
this focus point?

○———○———○———○———○———○———○———○———○———○
1   2   3   4   5   6   7   8   9   10
☹   ☺

This month's biggest wins

How good of a job did I do keeping
boundaries around my busy work?

○———○———○———○———○———○———○———○———○———○
1   2   3   4   5   6   7   8   9   10
☹   ☺

How do I feel about how I performed this
month, both from a financial and productivity
standpoint?

○———○———○———○———○———○———○———○———○———○
1   2   3   4   5   6   7   8   9   10
☹   ☺

This month's hardest lessons learned

What can I improve next month?

2020 PROGRESS

SEPTEMBER

FINANCIAL STAT	GOAL	RESULTS
SALES		
EXPENSES		
NET INCOME/LOSS		
PROFIT MARGIN PERCENTAGE		
NUMBER OF ORDERS		
VISITORS		
CONVERSION RATE		

SOCIAL MEDIA	STAT
FACEBOOK	
INSTAGRAM	
TWITTER	
PINTEREST	
EMAIL	
BLOG	

Why did you meet, exceed, or not meet your goals this month?

Did you pay yourself this month? If so, how much?

$

2020 PROGRESS

SEPTEMBER

Actions taken this month

Wedding

This month's bestselling products

This month's focus point was:

How good of a job did I do working on this focus point?

1   2   3   4   5   6   7   8   9   10
☹   ☺

This month's biggest wins

How good of a job did I do keeping boundaries around my busy work?

1   2   3   4   5   6   7   8   9   10
☹   ☺

How do I feel about how I performed this month, both from a financial and productivity standpoint?

1   2   3   4   5   6   7   8   9   10
☹   ☺

This month's hardest lessons learned

What can I improve next month?

2020 PROGRESS

QUARTERLY PLANNING

FINANCIAL STAT	GOAL QUARTERLY TOTAL	ACTUAL QUARTERLY TOTAL	NEED TO ADJUST ANNUAL GOAL?
SALES			
EXPENSES			
NET INCOME/LOSS			
PROFIT MARGIN PERCENTAGE			
NUMBER OF ORDERS			
VISITORS			
CONVERSION RATE			

Did you work on your focus points or did you get distracted with shiny objects?

Which strategies have seemed worth your time & energy and which have not?

2020 PROGRESS

QUARTERLY PLANNING

Patterns or trends I've noticed this quarter:

Financial Goals -
What do I need to adjust or change up next quarter?

Focus Points -
What do I need to adjust or change up next quarter?

2020 PROGRESS

OCTOBER

FINANCIAL STAT	GOAL	RESULTS
SALES		
EXPENSES		
NET INCOME/LOSS		
PROFIT MARGIN PERCENTAGE		
NUMBER OF ORDERS		
VISITORS		
CONVERSION RATE		

SOCIAL MEDIA	STAT
FACEBOOK	
INSTAGRAM	
TWITTER	
PINTEREST	
EMAIL	
BLOG	

Why did you meet, exceed, or not meet your goals this month?

Did you pay yourself this month? If so, how much?

$

2020 PROGRESS

OCTOBER

Actions taken this month

This month's bestselling products

This month's focus point was:

How good of a job did I do working on this focus point?

1   2   3   4   5   6   7   8   9   10

This month's biggest wins

How good of a job did I do keeping boundaries around my busy work?

1   2   3   4   5   6   7   8   9   10

This month's hardest lessons learned

How do I feel about how I performed this month, both from a financial and productivity standpoint?

1   2   3   4   5   6   7   8   9   10

What can I improve next month?

2020 PROGRESS

NOVEMBER

FINANCIAL STAT	GOAL	RESULTS
SALES		
EXPENSES		
NET INCOME/LOSS		
PROFIT MARGIN PERCENTAGE		
NUMBER OF ORDERS		
VISITORS		
CONVERSION RATE		

SOCIAL MEDIA	STAT
FACEBOOK	
INSTAGRAM	
TWITTER	
PINTEREST	
EMAIL	
BLOG	

Why did you meet, exceed, or not meet your goals this month?

Did you pay yourself this month? If so, how much?

$

2020 PROGRESS

NOVEMBER

Actions taken this month

This month's bestselling products

This month's focus point was:

How good of a job did I do working on
this focus point?

1   2   3   4   5   6   7   8   9   10
☹   ☺

This month's biggest wins

How good of a job did I do keeping
boundaries around my busy work?

1   2   3   4   5   6   7   8   9   10
☹   ☺

This month's hardest lessons learned

How do I feel about how I performed this
month, both from a financial and productivity
standpoint?

1   2   3   4   5   6   7   8   9   10
☹   ☺

What can I improve next month?

2020 PROGRESS

DECEMBER

FINANCIAL STAT	GOAL	RESULTS
SALES		
EXPENSES		
NET INCOME/LOSS		
PROFIT MARGIN PERCENTAGE		
NUMBER OF ORDERS		
VISITORS		
CONVERSION RATE		

SOCIAL MEDIA	STAT
FACEBOOK	
INSTAGRAM	
TWITTER	
PINTEREST	
EMAIL	
BLOG	

Why did you meet, exceed, or not meet your goals this month?

Did you pay yourself this month? If so, how much?

$

2020 PROGRESS

DECEMBER

Actions taken this month

This month's bestselling products

This month's focus point was:

How good of a job did I do working on this focus point?

○──○──○──○──○──○──○──○──○──○
1　2　3　4　5　6　7　8　9　10
☹　　　　　　　　　　　☺

This month's biggest wins

How good of a job did I do keeping boundaries around my busy work?

○──○──○──○──○──○──○──○──○──○
1　2　3　4　5　6　7　8　9　10
☹　　　　　　　　　　　☺

How do I feel about how I performed this month, both from a financial and productivity standpoint?

○──○──○──○──○──○──○──○──○──○
1　2　3　4　5　6　7　8　9　10
☹　　　　　　　　　　　☺

This month's hardest lessons learned

What can I improve next month?

2020 PROGRESS

TRACK YOUR TRAFFIC

Use this tracker to record your monthly traffic to your Etsy shop, self-hosted website, or other online venue. You can track monthly visitors or whichever particular traffic metric seems the most relevant for you. Tracking this data over time allows you to see if your marketing efforts are making an impact on your traffic. At the very least, you can establish traffic patterns and trends over seasons.

	ETSY	WEBSITE	
JANUARY			
FEBRUARY			
MARCH			
APRIL			
MAY			
JUNE			
JULY			
AUGUST			
SEPTEMBER			
OCTOBER			
NOVEMBER			
DECEMBER			
2020			

2020 VISITORS GOAL:

2020 PROGRESS

TRACK YOUR SALES

Use this tracker to record your monthly sales totals, number of orders, and take-home pay. Knowing whether you are on track to meet your targets throughout the year allows you to make changes and pivot as you go, rather than being surprised at year-end.

	SALES	NUMBER OF ORDERS	TAKE HOME PAY
JANUARY			
FEBRUARY			
MARCH			
APRIL			
MAY			
JUNE			
JULY			
AUGUST			
SEPTEMBER			
OCTOBER			
NOVEMBER			
DECEMBER			
2020			

2020 SALES GOAL:

2020 ORDERS GOAL:

2020 TAKE HOME PAY GOAL:

2020 PROGRESS

TRACK YOUR EXPENSES

Use this tracker to record your monthly spending. Let this info keep you on track with your budget!

	EXPENSES
JANUARY	
FEBRUARY	
MARCH	
APRIL	
MAY	
JUNE	
JULY	
AUGUST	
SEPTEMBER	
OCTOBER	
NOVEMBER	
DECEMBER	
2020	

2020 EXPENSE BUDGET:

2020 PROGRESS

TRACK YOUR PRODUCT SALES

You may find this tracker useful if you like to keep track of how many of each product type you sell throughout the year. This lets you see which products are selling the best and where you should focus your energy.

Product:

JANUARY		JULY	
FEBRUARY		AUGUST	
MARCH		SEPTEMBER	
APRIL		OCTOBER	
MAY		NOVEMBER	
JUNE		DECEMBER	

Product:

JANUARY		JULY	
FEBRUARY		AUGUST	
MARCH		SEPTEMBER	
APRIL		OCTOBER	
MAY		NOVEMBER	
JUNE		DECEMBER	

Product:

JANUARY		JULY	
FEBRUARY		AUGUST	
MARCH		SEPTEMBER	
APRIL		OCTOBER	
MAY		NOVEMBER	
JUNE		DECEMBER	

Product:

JANUARY		JULY	
FEBRUARY		AUGUST	
MARCH		SEPTEMBER	
APRIL		OCTOBER	
MAY		NOVEMBER	
JUNE		DECEMBER	

2020 PROGRESS

TRACK YOUR PRODUCT SALES

Product:

JANUARY		JULY	
FEBRUARY		AUGUST	
MARCH		SEPTEMBER	
APRIL		OCTOBER	
MAY		NOVEMBER	
JUNE		DECEMBER	

Product:

JANUARY		JULY	
FEBRUARY		AUGUST	
MARCH		SEPTEMBER	
APRIL		OCTOBER	
MAY		NOVEMBER	
JUNE		DECEMBER	

Product:

JANUARY		JULY	
FEBRUARY		AUGUST	
MARCH		SEPTEMBER	
APRIL		OCTOBER	
MAY		NOVEMBER	
JUNE		DECEMBER	

Product:

JANUARY		JULY	
FEBRUARY		AUGUST	
MARCH		SEPTEMBER	
APRIL		OCTOBER	
MAY		NOVEMBER	
JUNE		DECEMBER	

Product:

JANUARY		JULY	
FEBRUARY		AUGUST	
MARCH		SEPTEMBER	
APRIL		OCTOBER	
MAY		NOVEMBER	
JUNE		DECEMBER	

Product:

JANUARY		JULY	
FEBRUARY		AUGUST	
MARCH		SEPTEMBER	
APRIL		OCTOBER	
MAY		NOVEMBER	
JUNE		DECEMBER	

Here's to your success!

I genuinely hope you found the work you did in this Guidebook useful! We took the time to dig deep into what you really want to get out of your business. We set financial goals to express that, and we worked backwards from those goals to create an action plan for the year. Hopefully, you found this process enlightening and empowering.

Here's to a great 2020!

Make sure to join me in the Goal-Getting Maker group on Facebook where we can hone in on your goals even further and celebrate your success together!

WANT MORE FROM PAPER + SPARK®?

Visit me online at paperandspark.com and check out my bestselling bookkeeping spreadsheet templates and my free resource library.

Learn how to automate your shop, streamline your storefront, increase your productivity and focus more on the meaningful work with my course Asana for Makers at asanaformakers.com.

Get the details on everything you need to know to run the financial side of your business at paperandspark.com/2020GGG/

Questions or comments for me?
Contact me via email at hello@paperandspark.com.

Paper + Spark®

Made in the USA
Coppell, TX
24 August 2020

34176900R00077